The Guns of God

Equipping the Army of God for Victory

S0-AAZ-896

The Guns of God

Equipping the Army of God for Victory

George Otis
with Christine Darg

© Copyright 1997 — George Otis

All rights reserved. This book is protected under the copyright laws of the United States of America. This book may not be copied or reprinted for commercial gain or profit. The use of short quotations or occasional page copying for personal or group study is permitted and encouraged. Permission will be granted upon request. Unless otherwise identified, Scripture quotations are from the King James Version of the Bible. Scriptures marked NIV are from the New International Version®. NIV®. Copyright©, 1973, 1978, 1984 by International Bible Society. Emphasis within Scripture is the author's own.

Take note that the name satan and related names are not capitalized. We choose not to acknowledge him, even to the point of violating grammatical rules.

Treasure House

An Imprint of
Destiny Image® **Publishers, Inc.**
P.O. Box 310
Shippensburg, PA 17257-0310

"For where your treasure is,
there will your heart be also." Matthew 6:21

ISBN 1-56043-281-0

For Worldwide Distribution
Printed in the U.S.A.

First Printing: 1997   Second Printing: 1997

This book and all other Destiny Image, Revival Press,
and Treasure House books are available
at Christian bookstores and distributors worldwide.

For a U.S. bookstore nearest you, call **1-800-722-6774**.
For more information on foreign distributors, call **717-532-3040**.
Or reach us on the Internet: **http://www.reapernet.com**

Reach the author on the Internet:
http://www.highadventure.org

Dedication

This book is dedicated
to
Lucille Gravlee of Oklahoma.

God bless you
George Otis

Acknowledgments

The author wishes to acknowledge Christine Darg for her invaluable input during the formation of this book. Christine has authored three books of her own. She and her husband Peter represent High Adventure in Britain. Peter pioneered CBN's News Bureau in Jerusalem, and Christine wrote for *The Jerusalem Post.*

The author would also like to honor and acknowledge the valuable editorial contributions of Kathi Mills and the input and inspiration from Kris Gibbs.

A Call to Battle—A Call to Victory!

From Our Commander-in-Chief, the Lord of Hosts

"My children, I have called you, I have chosen you, I have anointed you, I have given you an instructed tongue. I have not done this to puff you up or give you glory, for I alone am your Glory. But I have called you and set you apart to be a mighty army, a victorious troop that will not fall nor retreat in the searing heat of battle.

"But, oh My children, you must understand that the enemy too has an army—vicious and ferocious—deceived, but determined to destroy you. He is mustering his troops, he is calling up his most powerful weapons, and the sound of battle is reverberating through the land.

"Because you are My chosen ones, the children of My heart, victory is assured. But hear My word to you! You cannot fight in the world—it is the enemy's territory. You must do battle in the Secret Place! You must put on the full armor I have provided you—and then stand in My righteousness. There is no other way.

"And that is why you are passing through hard places. I must make you know that man does not live by bread alone, but by every Word that proceeds from My mouth.

"I have put that Word in your mouth, and as you begin to dwell in the Secret Place, My Word will come forth from your mouth with the same power that created the heavens and the earth, and that raised Jesus from the dead. That Word will cut down the enemy where he stands, and will set the captives free.

"Draw near to Me, and I will draw near to you. Dwell in the Secret Place where the sound of My heartbeat will instruct you. I will not leave you or forsake you, for you are My children, the joy of My heart."

It is time to take the Kingdom
Rise up ye strong, 'tis Christ's command
For every power and every Kingdom
Is given now into your hand

He that hath ears to hear the Trumpet
He that hath heart to understand
It is the time to take the Kingdom
Rise up ye strong, possess the land.

Contents

Introduction xv

Chapter 1 Guns of God Duel the Guns of Hell. 1
Chapter 2 High Drama: Jerusalem to California. . . . 9
Chapter 3 Flesh and the Devil 17
Chapter 4 The Rusty Tanks 31
Chapter 5 Fighting the Good Fight 45
Chapter 6 From Theory to Action. 59
Chapter 7 Keeping Our Spiritual Guns Blazing 71
Chapter 8 The Rush Toward Eternity 79
Chapter 9 The Golden Sunrise! 85
Saga of the Chief Musician 91
Index of Scriptural Ammunition 93
Powerful Weapons for Victory 107
The Stars Are Falling 113
Recommended Reading 115
About the Author 117

Introduction

Mary Queen of Scots said, "I more fear the prayers of John Knox than all the armies of France."

When speaking of the power of prayer, the great Nobel Prize winner, Dr. Alex Carell declared, "Prayer is more powerful than 10,000 atom bombs."

Understanding the two types of prayer will help us better understand the power of prayer. There are two broad categories of prayer ministry: intercession, which is speaking to our Lord about needs, and spiritual warfare, which is entirely different. In intercessory prayer we are speaking to God. When we are waging spiritual warfare we are speaking to and attacking demonic forces by utilizing the Word of God. In the process of spiritual warfare we can bind the dark forces and loose the shackles they have put upon people and circumstances.

These two categories of prayer ministry are what I call the "Guns of God." The first category of the Guns of God, as I see it, are the voices God has given us to enter His throne room and intercede in prayer to Him on behalf of pressing earthly needs. The second category of the Guns of God is quite different. In this case our voices are dedicated to war directly against satan, the demonic hoards, and the fallen angels.

The powerful artillery to wage this war against these foes is the Word of God.

Jesus' dealings with satan and His prayers for the needy were indescribable in their effectiveness. He predominantly ministered through the words of His mouth. There is not an instance with the multitudes at Galilee when He did not heal them all, nor a time when He uttered words that did not produce miracles.

Little wonder indeed! History began when words were spoken that created mammoth planets, moons, stars, and galaxies covering a million light-years of the universe. Words alone set these spinning and hurled them into precision orbit. The universe was created, not by the scientist's "Big Bang," but by God's big word.

It is written, "When I consider Thy heavens, the work of Thy fingers..." (Ps. 8:3). That same power source comes down from the power lines of Heaven to allow us to live and act, through faith connection, in God's glory. Remember Jesus' promise to us, "And greater [things]... shall [you] do..." (Jn. 14:12b). He also promised, "...whatsoever ye shall ask in My name, that will I do" (Jn. 14:13a).

David destroyed the giant Goliath after declaring God's omnipotence. Samson, after a hasty prayer, took the jawbone of a donkey and killed 1,000 Philistines bent upon his murder.

Joshua, who was fighting time and facing an advancing enemy army, lifted his arm, spoke the Word, and stopped the sun. His own army prevailed, of course!

We know about Moses' prayers at the Red Sea. While a huge Egyptian army thundered down upon the children of Israel, the sea parted, the Israelites escaped, and the Egyptian army was drowned.

Jonathan and his armor-bearer faced a Philistine army of more than 100,000. He shot forth a Word of spiritual warfare: "It's no restraint of God to save by many or by few" (see 1 Sam. 14:6). God confirmed this radical truth and anointed these two young men to attack that entire army. History tells us that the enemy was utterly confused and destroyed. Never think that just you plus God aren't a majority over the enemy and over every problem. Jonathan tested this, and God has declared that He is no respecter of persons (see Acts 10:34b).

I am impressed with the power of God's Word and all the power He has entrusted us with in intercessory warfare. Now we must use it to bring in the final harvest of souls and prepare the way of the Lord.

Max Lucado writes in *Eye of the Storm*, "Conflict in this world is inevitable, but combat is optional." We have to choose to be warriors or to remain just dormant citizens freeloading in God's army.

At the back of this book we have placed an inventory of some of the surefire declarations given to us out of the mouth of God Himself. As you practice spiritual warfare, you can speak out these powerful Scriptures, one after another, as a crippling rebuke to these dark spirits.

We must remember that when Jesus was confronted by the devil himself He said, "It is written!" Jesus didn't rail at the devil and the demons or the fallen angels. He boldly spoke to them with authority, not yelling vile names. He knew yelling would be of little value and instead bound them, rebuked them, and loosed the people who were under their bondage; and that was it for these creatures.

When we engage in spiritual warfare against the satanic forces we are not to close our eyes or bow our heads. We are not praying to these creatures. We are binding and commanding them in Jesus' name. It is written, "[Before] the name of Jesus every knee [must] bow" (Phil. 2:10a).

Satan fell from Heaven like lightning and one-third of the creatures rebelled and came right behind him. One of the principal reasons for satan's failure and expulsion was his burning pride. That is why we do not bow our heads or close our eyes before him and his evil spirits. From this we can see the value of using the Word of God as an all-powerful weapon against the enemy; likewise, we can see the wisdom of avoiding bowing our heads before these creatures.

Remember too that it is not necessary to yell at these evil spirits but to boldly fire your Guns of God, sending forth the powerful bullets of the Word.

We will be binding and stopping the swarms of spirits in their tracks. The Lord said that in the last days satan would be going around "like a roaring lion" (see 1 Pet. 5:8 NIV); the opportunity to stop that roaring lion is now given to you and me to prepare the way of the Lord.

Before I go into a session of spiritual warfare against the enemy, there are some things I do. First, I speak to the Lord about my absolute love and confidence in Him. I then ask Him, as David did, to search me and try my heart and see if there be any wicked way in me, and to create within me a clean heart and renew a right spirit (see Ps. 139:23-24; 51:10-12).

Then I put on the whole armor of God (see Eph. 6:10-17). I pray aloud, and with my hands, in faith, put on these pieces of war equipment: the helmet of salvation, the breastplate of righteousness, the girdle of truth, and I shod my feet with the gospel of peace. Then I grasp the shield of faith with which to ward off all of the fiery darts of the enemy. With my other hand, in Jesus' name, I seize the sword of the Spirit, which is the Word of God.

John Greenleaf Whittier says, "So let it be in God's own might, we gird us for the coming fight, and, strong in Him whose cause is ours in conflict with unholy powers, we grasp the weapons He has given, The Light and Truth, and Love of Heaven."

Now you are a mighty warrior dressed for battle. If a Christian friend or your mate is available, carry on spiritual warfare against the devil together. The Bible tells us that one can put a thousand to flight, but two can put ten thousand to flight (see Deut. 32:30).

The types of targets to rise up against are the spirit of the enemy in our schools and universities and the spirits of evil in terrorist forces, driven by the one who comes to rob, to kill, and to destroy. Likewise, take part in spiritual warfare against spirits driving the pornographers, the child molesters, and the homosexual predators. Remember that we are not to participate in spiritual warfare by speaking the destruction of people in these evil realms. Our spiritual firepower is to be directed at the evil spirits driving them.

Other targets are the extremist cults like the one in Japan who worships the goddess of destruction; the spirits that promote violent youth gangs, the abortion movement, the drug pushers; the spirits swarming over Washington, DC, where our national leadership is based; the spirits of confusion, corruption, ignorance, and greed in political leaders.

These are but a few illustrations, but you can war wherever you see the enemy working—in your family, your business, your town, your state, your church, and on your job.

I'm really pleased that you have begun to read this book. One of the first precepts of winning a war is to know the enemy. Know the weapons you have to work with. Don't fear your enemy. God says, "No weapon that is formed against [you will] prosper" (Is. 54:17a).

Satan's seat is in the air. He is the "prince of the power of the air." (Eph. 2:2). A steady stream of the powerful declarations of God's Word weakens these forces tearing down our nation, our children, and our health. As you speak these words audibly, you are indeed preparing the way of the Lord, and He will come. You are advancing the timetable for His return from Heaven.

Chapter 1

Guns of God Duel
the Guns of Hell

The British jetliner cruised high above the rugged Yu-goslavian mountains en route to Israel. I stared out the window. The old brown King James lay open on my lap. It was mid-August of 1979, and the construction of the Voice of Hope radio station was nearing completion in Lebanon. *Would it be blown up before it was even born? Would it ever broadcast a hymn or a Scripture?* Such thoughts flowed through my mind as I thought about the work still to be done.

Beaufort Castle, the big PLO/Arafat Gibraltar of the Middle East, was a formidable obstacle to the completion of what we trusted would become the first-ever gospel station in the Holy Land—that is, if it ever made it. Beaufort was a major 850-year-old Crusader castle. Occupying an early Roman site, it commanded the Sidon-Damascus caravan route through the mountains. The castle's foundations were hewn out of solid rock of the lofty cliff above the Litani River.

From there the walls rose high above the ridge and boasted a thickness of more than 20 feet of stone near the parapet. Small wonder that Beaufort had easily withstood artillery and aerial bombardments through the years. Since the PLO had occupied the castle in the early 1970's, the Israelis often bombed and strafed it from the air. Major Haddad's Free Lebanese forces had also been shelling the structure, but all to no avail. PLO troops inside remained safe and free to terrorize Southern Lebanon and Galilee.

You see, the big PLO stronghold bristled with long-range cannon, heavy mortars, and Katyusha rocket launchers, that inflicted devastating casualties upon the people of southern Lebanon. And Beaufort was only one example of the PLO's ability to wreak destruction. Since their arrival in Lebanon fewer than nine years before, there had already been more than 70,000 casualties— Lebanese men, women, and children.

No wonder Lebanon was called "the land of wailing children and black-robed widows." The southern region of Lebanon lay almost dead in its ruins. The prophet Habakkuk had foreseen this very day when he wrote, "The violence you have done to Lebanon will overwhelm you" (Hab. 2:17a NIV).

As I sat there on the airliner speeding toward the Holy Land, I thought too of an article that had just been published by a PLO paper in Beirut about our Voice of Hope construction activities going on in the Valley of the Springs, which lay under Beaufort's guns. The article said, "This man Otis is naming his station 'The Voice of Hope,' but he should call it the 'Voice of Doom' because very soon we will blow it into oblivion!"

I shuddered. Our transmitters and antennae sat on open ground less than four miles east of Beaufort's guns and rockets. We were an easy target—a sitting duck—and now we had begun to attract their attention. By any human standard it would have been so easy for the PLO to carry out its threat. They were high and powerful, and we were lowly and defenseless.

Yet I knew God had led us to this place, and I felt reassured as I remembered that God often placed His people in situations of conflict where the odds were most unfavorable. I looked down at the Bible lying open on my lap and smiled. A small group of prayer warriors had been meeting in my home in Southern California on Tuesday evenings for several months now. The meetings often lasted three and four hours as we wrestled on our knees with the doubts and fears that assailed us in our quest for mountain-moving faith to accomplish our unusual and momentous goal. In this particular case, Beaufort was the mountain we needed moved.

It often happened during our sessions of prayer that one or another of the group would sense the leading of the Holy Spirit to a certain passage of Scripture pertaining to the matter about which we were praying. These passages would, in turn, often strike us with such a sense of holy mystery in their peculiar applicability that we would as a group affirm and receive them as specific messages from God to us in response to our prayers. Drawing from the Greek of the New Testament, we called them *rhemas*.

God had given us two *rhemas* about Beaufort. My Bible was open to one of them. It was in the fifth chapter of the book of the prophet Amos: "He who made the Pleiades and Orion...the Lord is His name—He flashes destruction on the stronghold and brings the fortified city to ruin" (Amos 5:8-9 NIV). The other passage was in Isaiah, chapter 26: "He humbles those who dwell on high, He lays the lofty city low; He levels it to the ground and casts it down to the dust" (Is. 26:5 NIV).

As I sat and contemplated these reassuring promises afresh, the Lord seemed to whisper, "Don't fret about Beaufort, for I Myself will deal with it—and yet this very year."

Wow!

Upon landing at Tel Aviv, I telephoned ahead to Metulla to arrange a meeting that same evening with Colonel Yoram Hamizrachi, the Israeli senior officer in the north, and Major Saad Haddad, Commander of Free Lebanon. I said, "Tell them I have some good news about their Beaufort problem."

Within four hours, Colonel Hamizrachi, Major Haddad, and I were huddled around coffee cups a few blocks from the Lebanese border at the Hotel Arazim in Metulla, Israel. The Major spoke first, "What's this about Beaufort?"

"You and your people have suffered enough from that stronghold," I explained. "The Lord has assured me He will silence Beaufort's guns before the year is out. I wanted you to hear it from me before it happens." I went on to tell them about the passages in Amos and Isaiah through which I believed God had spoken to me.

These two battle-hardened officers—one an Israeli and the other Lebanese—listened, but with understandable skepticism. Colonel Hamizrachi spoke first. "George, you're *ha'mashuga* [the crazy one]. The big old fort is impossible. Let's face it, she hasn't sat up there carved out of rock on a sheer 2,000-foot cliff for 850 years for nothing. It would take an atomic bomb to level her."

I did not try to defend what I had said. I simply knew I had heard from God and it involved good news for these two men and their suffering people. Only time would tell if I was right—or if I really was *ha'mashuga*.

Then the Israeli colonel hesitated and scratched his head. "George, I'll have to give you this much," he said. "I thought you were crazy last year when you prayed for rain here in Israel after our two years of drought. The rain came to us within two days." He smiled sheepishly. "So, tell me, how did God say He was going to do this and when will it happen?"

"I don't know any more than what I've told you," I replied. "But it will happen before this year is out, and it won't happen as a result of your weapons or some lucky shot, either."

The Major Haddad sighed. *"Inshala heer* [if God wills]. We'll see. We'll see."

Three weeks passed and I found myself on a sunny Thursday morning with our 20-man construction team who were working feverishly to complete the erection of our radio towers. The final sections of the second antenna were ready for installation. When "Stormy " Weathers, our antenna engineer, was finished, the two tall masts would each stand over 200 feet high. Our engineer, Paul Hunter, and our Lebanese technician, Charbel Younes, were struggling with a damaged transmitter over in the concrete electronics shack. Two other crews were laying 16 miles of #10 copper wire in little trenches, which ran out from the towers like the rays of the sun, to boost our ground conductivity. I was moving here and there, lending a hand where needed.

Spiritual Warfare in a Crisis Hour

Suddenly the earth heaved! A thunderous explosion rained shrapnel, rocks, dirt, and smoke on our site. Everyone hit the ground. A high-explosive shell from Beaufort had scored a direct hit on the corner of our site. Without thinking, I shot up from the ground, shook my fist toward the PLO fortress, and in what must have seemed a foolish gesture, I shouted, "That did it. Beaufort, you're finished!"

I whistled loudly to attract the attention of everyone on the site. Then I gestured to them to join me in the middle of the field. We held hands in an irregular circle, and I commenced to pray, "You know, Lord, that we cannot finish the Voice of Hope without Your protection. You promised to silence the cannons of this satanic fort this year, and we lovingly remind You and ask for immediate intervention. And so in the name of Jesus, you evil fort, we now take absolute authority over you and command your guns to be spiked. Your times of destruction and death are finished. On this very day, be bound and silenced. Amen."

Nothing happened.

We looked up from that prayer and headed back to our work spots. The big guns of Beaufort boomed again and again as if to mock us. But I clung to God's promise that "...the weapons of our warfare are not carnal, but mighty through God to the pulling down of strong holds" (2 Cor. 10:4). The 850-year-old fort was about to hear the Guns of God.

It was about ten o'clock in the morning when we stopped work for that little prayer meeting. The time ticked on and soon it was noon, time for a few of us to drive back to Metulla to pick up sandwiches at the Hotel Arazim as well as more construction supplies for our afternoon shift. We got into one of our rented vans and drove east up to the ridge overlooking the deep Litani River gorge.

As soon as we reached the ridge's crest, Beaufort came into view through our windshield. We could see it clearly. There was the illusion of being able to reach out and touch the death fortress standing just across the Litani but on its much higher western ridge.

I was sitting on the front seat of the van and glanced at my watch. It was 20 minutes past noon. When I looked back up I was greeted by a sight that none of us in that van will ever forget. Beaufort Castle suddenly "atomized" before our eyes. An explosive eruption shot fire and smoke, rocks and debris, gun barrels, artillery carriages, tires, rocket tubes, and shredded fragments hundreds and hundreds of feet into the air!

Awed and stunned, our driver pulled the van over to the side of the road. We all piled out and stood silently by the road while secondary explosions rumbled from inside the castle.

Then the scene fell silent as smoke continued to churn heavenward in thick billows. Almost simultaneously Paul Hunter and I shouted, "Praise the Lord!" And we all started cheering uncontrollably as if we had been rooting for an underdog football team that had just made the game-saving touchdown. Our prayers were being answered before our very eyes, clearly and unmistakably. None of us had ever before seen the power of God so dramatically demonstrated. I felt—there is no other word for it—jubilant. God had confirmed His Word and *Ha'mashuga*—the crazy one—had been privileged to see the arm of God's justice move. I suppose I had seemed a little crazy telling a couple of brave and experienced soldiers that God was going to single-handedly cripple their enemy's most powerful and impregnable stronghold. But I had taken the risk to speak it out weeks before knowing that our mighty God is dependable.

Spiritual warfare indeed. Nothing can withstand God's omnipotent Word!

Chapter 2

High Drama: Jerusalem to California

The Middle East adventure—as well as the title of this book—was birthed one morning in Jerusalem in the office of a powerful Israeli official.

"According to the Bible, what I am about to share with you could be termed the words of a prophet," I announced to that Israeli official. "Whether or not I'm a prophet, only God knows. But this I do know—the message I have for you is from God!"

The Israeli official was clearly intrigued. It's not every day that a ruler in Israel is visited by a Gentile with a message from God, but when it happened in the Bible, it was always a significant moment in the history of God's people.

Israel—now reborn after nearly 2,000 years of dispersion—was in deep trouble once again. Her leaders were, as in the days of the Judges, "doing what seemed right in their own eyes," in desperate, last-ditch attempts to make peace with her enemies. War-weary, shell-shocked, and beleaguered by the elusive process of peace, Israel was still vulnerable to being obliterated by her many enemies. But God's invisible hand was holding back the carnage threatened by Islamic terrorists.

Yet God's principles are ever true: "Surely the Lord God will do nothing, but He revealeth His secret unto His servants the prophets" (Amos 3:7). And I had heard from the Lord.

The leader cordially offered me a seat for what proved to be a fascinating meeting, one which ultimately lasted several hours. He said, "What's on your mind today, George?"

I answered, "Your enemies are shortly going to outgun you, humanly speaking, if you try to stand up against them in your own strength." I continued, "Even the weapons out at Diamona can't save Israel. But if you will give us permission to put a Voice of Hope relay station somewhere near Jerusalem, something will come of it for Israel."

"What's that?" the official asked, raising his eyebrow questioningly. He'd already sat at hundreds of negotiating tables, endured countless diplomats, and was disciplined as a good soldier never to be too surprised at anything he heard.

I blurted out, "We shall use the *Guns of God* on Israel's behalf! Your enemies may outgun you in the natural, but by using the Guns of God, the enemy will be stopped!"

It was the first time that loaded phrase—the "Guns of God"—bubbled up out of my spirit and out of my mouth. *The Guns of God! The Guns of God!* Yes, even as I prophesied it, those words had a ring of truth, a ring of justice, a ring of authority, a sound of security for Israel in her desperation.

"What are the Guns of God?" the official asked, with a slight trace of a smile on his lips.

I thought to myself, *Well, here goes. Either he hears what the Spirit is saying or he misses it. Thank God my duty is only to be faithful as a watchman, as Ezekiel was.*

I took a deep breath and dove in. "Do you believe that there's a devil and that there are hosts of wicked spirits who are hell-bent on destroying the Jews?"

The question didn't seem to perturb the Israeli; in fact, it seemed to answer some half-formed question he'd been pondering for years for which the answer had always eluded him. "Well, after all we've been through," he acquiesced, "we have to believe that there really are devils."

"Those demons mean to destroy Israel," I said. (He shared with me later that he felt something like a mantle coming down upon him even as I spoke.) "But we have the Guns of God, that is, the all-powerful Word of God. We can use our powerful broadcast stations to bind these demons with the Word of God, which the Bible calls the 'sword of the Spirit.' Believe me, the Word of God is powerful ammunition. It is living and it is very active. It is more powerful than a nuclear weapon, and it is your best defense. The Lord wants me to use it on behalf of Israel. The devil's office is in the sky. The Bible calls him the 'prince of the power of the air' (See Eph. 2:2). We can power up to be more effective to wage spiritual war, to push back those powers of darkness on your behalf."

I took a deep breath and looked the Israeli in the eye. "The Word of God and we believers are your allies. The more land you have given to your enemies to buy peace, the more danger you are in. God made an eternal covenant with Israel on that land. You have no right to give it away! Remember that the Bible says, 'Today they cry peace, peace, then sudden destruction' " (see 1 Thess. 5:3).

"Do you think it will work?" he asked.

What a question!

I answered, "I not only *think* it will work, I *know* it will work!"

I quickly recounted how the Voice of Hope Network had already been waging spiritual warfare over various hot spots and had seen that the strategy of sending forth God's Word really works.

There was the Rwanda crisis. Before the TV cameras of the world, we recoiled in horror as demon-possessed people were killing and mutilating other tribesmen and mercilessly decapitating babies. It was more than inhuman; it was clearly demonically inspired and controlled. High Adventure turned their most powerful transmitter toward that East African nation and sent forth powerful proclamations of the Word of God against the demonic hosts that were literally butchering that nation. Within less than two weeks of the spiritual warfare broadcasts, the carnage suddenly ceased.

I shared with the Israeli official, "Those demons had to flee. They could not withstand that Word of God coming at them. You must understand that in spiritual warfare we are not broadcasting to people or dealing at all with politics. We are dealing with the dark forces controlling people through politics, military, or whatever other means! We are not against people. This is not a warfare of flesh and blood. The Bible tells us we are not dealing with people, but with dark powers and principalities (See Eph. 6:12)."

I also shared with the official how the elections in America had taken an about-face after the spiritual warfare

High Adventure had broadcast into the nation's capital, which had become a murder capital full of corruption and every vile act sanctioned by the government.

"If only broadcasting tools had been available to us when Hitler and his hoards were slaughtering millions of Jews under the direct inspiration of satan," I said, "we could have turned the Guns of God toward the holocaust perpetrators. But now this tool and strategy has been put into our hands, and we dare not ignore the solemn responsibility we have to use God's Word on behalf of God's people, if you will let us!"

I shook the official's hand to say "Shalom." He left me with the blessing to conduct spiritual warfare on behalf of Israel in the heavenlies. It was a day of unprecedented revelation.

What an awesome day we are destined to live in, when we as believers can stand as intercessors in the gap on behalf of the people of God to keep them from being decimated by her enemies. Israel is not able, at this point in time, to believe for herself, because the Holy Spirit has not yet been poured out on her resurrected "dry bones." For this reason Israel continues to be vulnerable and we must war in prayer for her.

But we believers who know our God can be strong and do exploits on Israel's behalf (see Dan. 11:32). As intercessors standing in the gap in the airwaves, we can believe on her behalf until she can believe for herself. The honor of the Lord's name is ultimately at stake. It is His throne and His Word that are besmirched every time Israel is threatened to be cast into the sea.

Like Aaron and Hur, we must hold up the arms of Moses (representing Israel) so that Israel can continue to survive her battles until that great day prophesied by Zechariah, when Israel shall look with believing faith upon the Pierced One (see Jn. 19:37).

God's people are waking up to the fact that we are now empowered and are engaged in a war. While I spoke and prophesied to the Israeli official, Christine Darg had the privilege of holding conferences in England and in Israel to believe God for the pushing back of the powers of darkness over the Middle East, based on Psalm 83 and 68:

O God, do not keep silent; be not quiet, O God, be not still. See how Your enemies are astir, how Your foes rear their heads. With cunning they conspire against Your people; they plot against those You cherish. "Come," they say, "let us destroy them as a nation, that the name of Israel be remembered no more." With one mind they plot together; they form an alliance against You...with the people of Tyre. Even Assyria has joined them to lend strength... (Psalm 83:1-8 NIV).

What can be done when we see these things being fulfilled before our eyes? We are not dealing with politics or human beings but with the counsels of hell, which are plotting to defame God's name and eternal purposes by trying to destroy His people and His heritage. There is an answer:

Let God arise, let His enemies be scattered: let them also that hate Him flee before Him. As smoke is driven away, so drive them away: as wax melteth before the fire, so let the wicked perish at the presence of God. ... Sing unto God, sing praises to His name: extol Him that rideth upon the heavens by His name JAH, and rejoice before Him (Psalm 68:1-2,4).

So we see that jubilant praise and singing can create a highway in the deserts of the Middle East for God Himself to move onto the scene and to scatter His enemies in the demonic realms. As it is also written in Psalm 149, we have learned that joyful, high praises are powerful ammunition. They are some of the mighty Guns of God!

Let the high praises of God be in their mouth, and a twoedged sword in their hand; to execute vengeance upon the heathen, and punishments upon the people; to bind their [spiritual] *kings with chains, and their nobles with fetters of iron; to execute upon them the judgment written...* (Psalm 149:6-9).

Chapter 3

Flesh and the Devil

Before we get too far into our teaching about using the Guns of God, I feel it is important to point out the difference between the flesh and the devil. You see, it is God's design that Christians really know the tactics and all of the insidious ways of satan and his cohorts. It is of equal importance that they be aware of the "works of the flesh." Sometimes these are confused. Some Christians seem to behave as though the fruitage of their own undisciplined will is all from demonic action in their life—"the devil made me do it" syndrome. Take Scott, for example.

Although Scott was born again, he had never invested any time or effort into growing in the things of God. He enjoyed the emotional high he experienced when involved in praise and worship services. He even commented on how good he felt when he would leave church on Sunday mornings. But he just couldn't seem to hold on to that "feel-good" during the week.

Without his emotional high to keep him on track, Scott found himself sinking deeper and deeper into cynicism and unbelief. When a Christian brother lovingly confronted him and suggested he needed to learn to discipline his flesh and renew his mind through daily Bible reading and prayer, he became very defensive. His problems weren't due to his lack of discipline, he insisted; they were because the devil was attacking him and trying to make him miserable. In fact, he was upset with his friend for not offering to bind the devil's working in his life, rather than suggesting that the problem might be due to his flesh.

Scott's is a classic case of confusing the works of the flesh and the works of the devil. Without a doubt, the devil is working overtime to bring destruction at every possible opportunity, and he will gladly take advantage of a weak-flesh situation like Scott's. But we must remember that not all problems can be blamed on the devil. Many of our problems and failures can be attributed to our own lack of self-discipline and self-control.

When believers try to cure these fleshly problems by exorcism, they will always meet with failure. Indeed, confusion and personal hurt can be caused by such faulty diagnosis.

Seeking deliverance may sound like an easy out for those who find it difficult to exercise discipline. Some fail to repent of their own sowing to the flesh, which allowed that foothold to the enemy in the first place. We see tormented people who continually go to "deliverance meetings," refusing to develop their Christian disciplines and responsibilities of life. The Bible says to "lay aside every weight, and the sin which doth so easily beset us, and let us run with patience the race that is set before us" (Heb. 12:1b).

Many problems that Christians face have a natural explanation. Some are due to the pull of our flesh or self-life. We may call these "bad habits." Paul tells us to "Likewise reckon ye also yourselves to be dead indeed unto sin" (Rom. 6:11a) and "...make not provision for the flesh, to fulfill the lusts thereof" (Rom 13:14). There is no easy substitute for discipline in the Christian life. Those desirous of "flip" remedies will find repeated disappointments. They will experience soaring victory in a deliverance meeting one night and then crash in "Dismal Valley" the next day.

Even though we can't do it in our own strength, we do have a vital part in this spiritual walk of victory. It's a "joint venture" with God. We must be determined to walk in righteousness and then He will supply the power for us to do so.

The works of the flesh will never be eliminated by trying to cast them out as evil spirits. Our old man or sin nature is crucified with Jesus "that the body of sin might be destroyed..." (Rom. 6:6b). Put it this way: "Let us never forget that our old selves died with Him on the cross, that the tyranny of sin over us might be broken, for a dead man can safely be said to be immune to the power of sin" (**version). From this you can see that our part is to "reckon" it done and then purpose to live accordingly.

Have you ever known believers who are overly demon conscious? The devil really doesn't mind being slandered, just as long as people talk about him and his works. He likes for Christians to witness about his "mighty deeds," to attribute our frailties of will and all our woes to him. This gives him undeserved attention.

Now, we aren't to be ignorant of satan's devices, but he isn't to be the centerpiece of our thoughts or conversation.

As we lift up Jesus in our lives and with our words, He will draw men to Himself. We are to be "looking unto Jesus the author and finisher of our faith" (Heb. 12:2a).

This book has been written to illuminate satan's jet-age strategies and provide triumph over them. But to maintain spiritual balance, we must also stress the big role that our own will plays. Let's follow Paul's injunction to "fight the good fight of faith" (1 Tim. 6:12a) by turning from sinful indulgences and instead following after righteousness, godliness, faith, love, and patience. It is also most imperative that we break away from our old friends who have exposed us to temptations.

You know, it's so easy to "tilt with windmills," as poor Don Quixote did. Today, as the Spirit is quickening many to a new awareness of satan, we must guard against going too far the other way. Some churches have suffered from years of neglect in teaching the reality of satan and God's victory provisions. But we must keep the pendulum from swinging to the other extreme now that his reality is established. After all, he isn't all powerful, and we should not give him credit for things he can't do. It is also important that we avoid using him as an excuse for all of our own failures. Too often sins stemming from an undisciplined will are rationalized away as satan's doings. God said no temptation would be able to overtake us from which He would not provide a way of escape (see 1 Cor. 10:13). Therefore, it is clear that we have the means to overcome sin. Let's take another look at what the Bible says about the works of the flesh.

For the flesh lusteth against the Spirit, and the Spirit against the flesh: and these are contrary the one to the other…. Now the works of the flesh are manifest, which are these; Adultery, fornication, uncleanness, lasciviousness, idolatry, witchcraft, hatred, variance, emulations [jealousy], *wrath, strife, seditions* [stirring up rebellion, party spirit], *heresies, envyings, murders, drunkenness, revellings, and such…* (Galatians 5:17,19-21).

Let's face it. We just aren't able to cast ourselves out of those works of the flesh either. The sooner Christians grasp this, the quicker the Holy Spirit can start developing the strength for resistance in our own wills.

The Bible tells us to resist those sin appetites stemming from our carnal flesh. "Let not sin therefore reign in your mortal body, that ye should obey it in the lusts thereof. Neither yield ye your members as instruments of unrighteousness unto sin: but yield yourselves unto God…" (Rom. 6:12-13). It is clear from the study of Romans and other Scripture passages that new creatures in Christ can live free from the bondage of sin *if they choose to avail themselves of Gods power and provision to do so.*

In Ephesians there is a powerful key to the victorious Christian life: "Put on the whole armour of God, that ye may be able to stand against the wiles of the devil. For we wrestle not against flesh and blood, but against principalities, against powers, against the rulers of the darkness of this world, against spiritual wickedness in high places" (Eph. 6:11-12).

How can we know whether sinning stems from our own weak will or from external demonic forces? Here are a couple of telltale indicators:

1. Are we being repetitiously driven?

2. Is there an abnormality in our behavior or something that consumes our healthy, normal personality?

The nature of satan is abnormality. Some have slowly adjusted to abnormal behavior by saying that it is just a part of their personality. Maybe they have rationalized certain quirks as inherited weakness. But Scripture promises us the potential to walk in newness of His life and that it is available for every aspect of our existence.

There are three ways that evil spirits employ to bring wreckage or captivity: oppression, obsession, and possession. Matthew 12 and Mark 5 clearly indicate that demons have no rest unless they can satisfy their own appetites, lusts, and desires. They are looking for spiritually careless persons who will, through continual sin, provide an opening for them. But Jesus came to free such as are oppressed by the devil.

"...God anointed Jesus of Nazareth with the Holy Ghost and with power: who went about doing good, and healing all that were oppressed of the devil..." (Acts 10:38). To oppress means to exercise dominion against one, to weigh heavily on the mind. The Bible tells how "there came also a multitude out of the cities round about unto Jerusalem, bringing sick folks, and them which were vexed with unclean spirits: and they were healed every one" (Acts 5:16).

Obsession is another way satan attacks mankind. The word *obsess* means to vex, harass, or to haunt. These assaults are focused on the mind or thought life. Watchman Nee in *Spiritual Man* writes about the believer's mind:

"Even following repentance the believer's mind is not liberated totally from a touch by Satan. As the enemy worked through the mind in former days, so today will he work in the same manner. Paul, in writing to the Corinthian believers, confided that he was afraid, that as the serpent deceived Eve by his cunning, their thoughts would be led astray from a sincere and pure devotion to Christ (see 2 Cor. 11:3). The Apostle well recognized that, as the god of this world blinds the mind of unbelievers, so will he deceive the mind of the believers. Even though they are saved, their life of thought is as yet unrenewed; consequently it remains the most strategic battleground. The mind suffers the onslaughts of the powers of darkness more than any other organ of the whole man.

"Paul warns of one of those ways a wrong spirit can come: 'If someone comes and preaches another Jesus than the one we preached, or if you received a different spirit from the one we received, or if you accept a different gospel from the one you accepted.' The peril for the Christian is to have false teaching injected into his thought life so as to lead him astray from a sincere and pure devotion to Christ. These are the works the 'serpent' is perpetrating today. Satan has disguised himself as an angel of light to lead saints to worship with their intellect a Jesus other than the Lord, to receive a spirit other than the Holy Spirit, and by these to propagate a gospel other than the gospel of the grace of God."

God's shield against the "dart of obsession" is to be used at the very threshold of our imagination. One of God's sure ways to lick this kind of obsession is by "casting down imaginations, and every high thing that exalteth itself against the knowledge of God, and bringing into captivity every thought to the obedience of Christ" (2 Cor. 10:5). It is also important not to watch, read, or listen to inflaming things.

Just as God desires the believer to be filled with the Holy Spirit, satan's intent and desire is that mankind be demon-possessed. Satan would like to have people think evil spirits are a figment of ignorant people's imaginations or some joke. But the Bible doesn't laugh about evil spirits. "For unclean spirits, crying with loud voice, came out of many that were possessed with them" (Acts 8:7a).

A wise and experienced minister, the Reverend E. Burnette, in his booklet *Is Demon Power Real Today?* writes:

"The Holy Spirit dwells in a man's spirit, and a demon can dwell in an area of the body. This can cause an infirmity and mental sickness, too. A demon can attach itself to an area of the physical body and possess or hold sway over it. If a man was blind and dumb (and the cause of it was demonic—and it certainly isn't in all cases) that part of him would be possessed with a demon. Possession simply means that there is a certain area of the body that is dominated by satanic power" (see Mt. 12,15).

Well then, can Christians actually be possessed or demonized? The Bible clearly shows that demons can occupy human bodies (see 1 Tim. 4 and 1 Jn. 4). The First Timothy account says that individuals who were once in the faith had fallen away only to be seduced by evil spirits.

Burnette gives this allegory:

"The Jewish temple is made up of three parts: the outer court, the inner court, and the Holy of Holies. God dwells, of course, in the Holy of Holies. This Jewish man, knowing better, brought cows, sheep, doves, and set up tables and gambled and defiled the temple. The Lord came and drove them all out and said, 'Make not my Father's house a house of merchandise.'

"They weren't in the Holy of Holies, but the moment these animals, etc., were brought in, they defiled the outer court, or the body."

The Bible warns: "Neither give place to the devil" (Eph. 4:27). No believer can expect to willfully and repetitiously sin against God without the enemy sooner or later having a foothold to oppress, vex, or bind him.

Sometimes those with demonic oppression, obsession, or possession are described as having natural or organic disorders. Some describe them as complexes, delusions, depression, psychoneurosis, compulsions, and the like. But permanent cure can be realized only through spiritually correct methods.

We need to watch every area of our lives that is repeatedly fought over by the adversary. It is good for each of us to ask God to show us hidden danger spots. David prayed, "Search me, O God, and know my heart: try me, and know my thoughts: and see if there be any wicked way in me, and lead me in the way everlasting" (Ps. 139:23-24). But why is this important? We should nip in the bud any opening for satan before it becomes too much for us to handle. The Bible puts it this way: "But every man is tempted, when he is drawn away of his own lust, and enticed. Then when lust hath conceived, it bringeth forth sin: and sin, when it is finished, bringeth forth death" (Jas. 1:14-15).

Jesus' ministry proved again and again the reality of evil spirits. He came to destroy the works of the devil. Let's watch Jesus at work:

Jesus stood over Peter's mother-in-law and "rebuked the fever; and it left her: and immediately she arose and ministered unto them" (Lk. 4:39). Note here that He didn't heal her from some natural problem causing fever, but that He rebuked a spirit. It was a malevolent "being" that was causing her fever. Here are a few other Scripture proofs:

> *And ought not this woman, being a daughter of Abraham, whom Satan hath bound, lo, these eighteen years, be loosed from this bond...?* (Luke 13:16)

> *...There met Him out of the tombs a man with an unclean spirit. ... For He said unto him, Come out of the man, thou unclean spirit* (Mark 5:2,8).

> *They brought unto Him all that were diseased, and them that were possessed with devils. ... And He healed many that were sick of divers diseases, and cast out many devils...* (Mark 1:32b,34).

Now let's notice Jesus Himself differentiating between those who were demon possessed and others who were sick:

> *...They brought unto Him many that were possessed with devils: and He cast out the spirits with His word, and healed all that were sick* (Matthew 8:16).

It is quite clear that in certain cases physical and mental problems are caused by evil spirits. One example is the case of the father who brought his son to Jesus. The father said the boy was a "...lunatick, and sore vexed: for ofttimes he falleth into the fire, and oft into the water. ... And Jesus rebuked the devil; and he departed out of him: and the child was cured from that very hour" (Mt. 17:15,18).

Then was brought unto Him one possessed with a devil, blind, and dumb: and He healed him, insomuch that the blind and dumb both spake and saw (Matthew 12:22).

Now let's review some suggested rules for victorious living recently shared by "Revival Time" speaker C.M. Ward. These may be helpful in bringing our heart attitudes into line before we pray for God's intervention in our problems:

1. Don't shift the blame. First Corinthians 11:28a says, "But let a man examine *himself.*" Most of our troubles are of our own making.
2. Don't make excuses. Alibis are distasteful to God. Confess your faults if you want to be rid of them (see Jas. 5:16; 1 Jn. 1:9).
3. Don't dodge (or evade) the issues.

The whole matter of evading the issue, shifting the blame, or passing the buck is basically a position of cowardice. The Bible is rich with examples of those who violated these principles. They may help us to avoid similar snares.

Adam whimpered that it was really God's fault and Eve's. Listen to him: "...The woman whom Thou gavest to be with me, she gave me of the tree..." (Gen. 3:12).

Then there was Cain's complaint. He refused to look in the mirror at himself. "My punishment is greater than I can bear. Behold, Thou hast driven me out this day from the face of the earth..." (Gen. 4:13b-14). He was saying that God was too harsh in His dealings and unreasonable in His judgments; but he made no mention of his own sins of jealousy, arrogance, rebellion, and even murder.

In the beginning God created male and female—one for one. But Lamech was the first person who disregarded this arrangement. He took to himself two wives. One day he came in after a fight and tried to justify his actions: "I have killed a man for wounding me," he declared. "But if Cain got away with murder, then I, Lamech, should seventy times more" (see Gen. 4:23-24). This is a good picture of self-justification without one word of sorrow for what he had done. Pointing to someone else's sin, which seems worse than ours, is still a common dodge.

The Bible heroes with vain excuses have been exposed, as we see, for our instruction. So will it be with us if we try to excuse our own sin. God still doesn't forgive alibis.

The blood of the Lamb is the remedy for our sins. We must admit our sins before we can be cleansed. Never rationalize them; if we do, we will be exposing ourselves to the stalking lion's claws. But there is a place of refuge for God's children even in this difficult earth life. That sole refuge is found in that same One who said, "I am the way, the truth, and the life…" (Jn. 14:6b).

If after reading this chapter, you feel that the problems you are wrestling with are definitely demonic rather than simply undisciplined flesh, or because of an ongoing sin in your life you have given satan a foothold, then look at these ways to cope with these demonic forces once and for all.

Identify the source of your problem. Pinpoint when and where satan gained control over that area of your life.

Confession. Name it for what it is. Don't make any excuses.

Battle that thing which opened the door. Make God's enemies your enemies (see Ps. 139).

Renounce it out loud. You don't need to be polite to satan. Command him to leave in Jesus' name. Remember, you have willingly let him in, and he will not leave unless you command him to do so. If there is reluctance on your part, he will hold on. But he has to bow before the name of Jesus and must leave at your command.

Break all former associations with anything that is tainted. This includes wrong friends, cult churches, and old hangouts. Destroy all literature, paraphernalia, idols, and so forth (see Acts 19). Never go back to the people or the places where you were enslaved. Satan would like to draw you back into that bondage if he could. This is an extremely important point as a young lady named Julie learned so vividly.

Julie was raised in an alcoholic family, and by the age of 17, had become an alcoholic herself. At 25, homeless and alone, Julie responded to the gospel presented to her by a group of believers witnessing on the street in front of a bar she frequented. Not only was she gloriously saved and delivered, but the group took her in and helped her find a job and an apartment. Two years later, however, she was back on the streets, homeless and drunk once again.

What happened? Did God fail her? Did demons pull her back into sin against her will? Of course not! God had indeed set her free, but her flesh was weak; and against the advice and counsel of Christian brothers and sisters, she began to associate with old friends and stop in at her once favorite hangouts telling herself she could "handle it" now that she was a Christian. Obviously, she was wrong. When God sets us free from sin, we are never to compromise with that and go back, for if we do, the Bible warns us that we will end up in worse shape than we were in before (see Mt. 12:43-45).

Be loosed. If you're under the dominion of another through sorcery, hypnotism, psychic powers, curses, and so forth, you must throw off the source of that dominion. You must be loosed from it. Speak it out. Jesus said that "whatsoever thou shalt loose on earth shall be loosed in heaven" (Mt. 16:19b).

Spiritual domination over another person is really satan's power working through that person. It can be broken by prayer; then start "bringing into captivity every thought to the obedience of Christ" (2 Cor. 10:5b).

Fill that which is empty. "Be filled with the Spirit" (Eph. 5:18b). Feed on the Word. We are strongest in our faith after hearing the Word of God. Fellowship and pray with Christians frequently.

There is but one Deliverer—your Advocate, Jesus Christ. And He said, "Him that cometh to me I will in no wise cast out" (Jn 6:37b).

Finally, **stand and withstand**. We are to stand against all the wiles of the enemy and are promised that if we resist the devil, he will flee from us. Resisting through the power of the Holy Spirit is your responsibility now. He is out—so keep him out!

Victory is your rightful portion. Through Jesus' work on the cross, you have just traded spiritual impotence for triumphant living!

Now let's move on in our study of the Guns of God—the surefire way to defeat the enemy and to continue in victory!

Chapter 4

The Rusty Tanks

It was startling! The vision, I mean. Only once before had I ever heard from the Lord through a vision. Suddenly, I was looking through a large, round porthole as if from inside a ship. My eyes became wide at the awesome sight that met me. For miles in every direction there were tens of thousands of the latest, most sophisticated, and powerful weapons of war I had ever seen. Military tanks, rocket launchers, warships, huge missiles, Stealth fighter planes, and supersonic bombers. On and on it went.

It took my breath away to see such a war arsenal! Enough power to conquer the whole world and then some. I said to the Lord, "What does this mean? What is all that rust?" He answered, "Come and I will show you." In the Spirit the Lord carried me back and forth across this terrible fleet of great war machines and weapons.

As we drew closer I exclaimed, "Why, they're *all* rusting!"

The Spirit said, "I will interpret the vision for you."

The Lord began to answer a swirl of questions that came into my heart. We Christians have been magnificently empowered by Heaven to:

ONE: Overcome our enemy;
TWO: Prepare for the return of the Lord;
THREE: Bring in the final harvest of souls.

No other generation has been blessed with tools such as these: fine churches, strong preachers, musicians, books, Bibles and magazines flowing like a fountain, gospel radio and TV programs from coast to coast.

Then the Spirit of the Lord said, "I am the Captain of the Lord of Hosts. The next battle will be our last. I have issued each the weapons and the armor to overcome the forces of darkness, but I don't have the standing army I need. Too often it instead is a 'standing-around' army. There is a gypsy quality in some believers who race from meeting to meeting instead of engaging the enemy. Haven't I said, 'Even the gates of hell shall not prevail against you'?"

Today we lack for nothing. But we aren't using the spiritual weapons so lavishly heaped upon us by the Lord. Our God-given "tanks" are just sitting there, largely unused and rusting. Remember, the early disciples had none of these but even so they "turned the world upside down" (see Acts 17:6). We are arrayed and empowered against the vast army led by satan. Our battle orders call for us to subdue the enemy and to set the captives free. We have enough "fire power" to turn the world upside down again.

The final harvest is now at our feet, but who can overcome Satan's millions of unseen dark spirits blocking our path? We can! Our Lord ordained us for spiritual warfare when He proclaimed, "...I give unto you power...over all the power of the enemy" (Luke 10:19a). In my vision of the rusting tanks, God was saying to His Church, "I've even given you more weapons than you need to bring a swift and final victory, but most of these are being left to rust by My people." We can finish preparing the way of the Lord, but it's not enough to talk about our weapons and study them. It's time to use them.

God is asking, "Who will run for Me and leap into those spiritual tanks? Who will drive for Me these chariots of fire?" Let us be swift to answer, "Here am I, Lord, send me!"

Let us study for a moment just one of the most powerful weapons God has put in our hands for bringing this age to a close. Spiritual warfare has been sinfully neglected. It is a type of prayer where we do not speak to God, but rather confront the enemy with the Word.

When we pray, we always talk to the Lord about our wants and needs. We ask for help in our marriages, our health, our finances, our churches, our children, and our country. We pray intercessory prayers for others. But now let's consider for a moment this powerful unused weapon that God has put into our hands to shake the kingdom of darkness.

Spiritual warfare is declaring to satan, his fallen angels, demons, and evil spirits the absolute authority of God over them. Jesus rebuked spirits and commanded them to come out. Jesus also did this when He commanded the sickness to come out of Peter's mother; in the case of the child who was thrown into the fire during a fit; and when He cast a thousand demons out of the man from Gadarenes. Jesus, who along Galilee healed thousands and performed uncounted miracles, said, "And greater things shall you do" (see Jn. 14:12).

To hasten the coming of Jesus we must continue to increase our intercessory prayers, but we must also launch spiritual warfare using God's Word. When we see satanic forces working in our schools, in our nation, in sickness, in wars, in our children, and in our finances, we must send forth a volley of binding, overcoming declarations to stop the enemy in his tracks.

If this sounds radical, well it is! War *is* radical. War done in the power of Jesus, our Captain, is radical. And we have within our capability a level of power that God wants us to tap in on to hasten the coming of the Kingdom.

High Adventure has declared spiritual warfare in a number of world situations over the past year. We have seen glorious and awesome results. God's Word truly is quick and powerful and sharper than any two-edged sword.

We did so on behalf of Cuba and Haiti, and today we see tremendous evidences of God's Word being triumphant over evil in those countries. We also undertook an intensive spiritual warfare campaign into Washington, DC. With the Word of God we fought against the demonic forces swarming over our national capital, bringing about corruption, crime, evil, and waste. The moral atmosphere in Washington began to change! We broadcast the Word right into satan's domain because he is the prince of the power of the air!

Now these are recent campaigns of "Strategic Spiritual Warfare" using powerful transmitters on behalf of nations and cities. But you can personally use spiritual warfare against sickness, poverty, oppression for your family, church, or community. Is the work all done? Not yet, but what a start!

The Guns of God

You might think this will cause us to neglect the evangelical broadcasting we have always followed. Not so, but we are committed, until Jesus returns, to follow His proven spiritual course. On all ten of our stations, which are strategically placed around the world, we shall sustain intensive broadcast programs with prayers for the sick and calls to accept Jesus; teaching programs of encouragement and hope; teaching programs of deliverance for those in the radio congregation suffering from demonic oppression; and, of course, continuing to proclaim the Word of God!

This ministry direction we have maintained is now bringing an enormous harvest. Listeners in every continent of the world are writing to testify of their salvation, deliverance, miracles, healings, and miraculous release from pains and mental problems. This new surge of harvest is the single most thrilling experience of my entire life.

When we first received the Lord's command to add spiritual warfare on top of all our regular ministry, we asked, "But how can we do it? When can we do it? We have such a heavy schedule." The Spirit quickly answered, "By weakening the enemy with My Word you will then see the last revival follow and the beginning of the final harvest. Spiritual warfare is My strategy, and you can do it every night without interfering at all with your daytime minutes!"

Warfare for the Nations

The devil struck in the heart of Africa. Millions watched on television as thousands of Rwandans butchered each other week after week. Babies were beheaded and women slaughtered. As multitudes of Rwandans fled in terror toward neighboring Zaire, they were pursued by demon-possessed men who butchered them.

After watching this ghastly carnage, the Lord revealed something startling. All the world's armies, all the world's diplomats, and all the world's relief agencies could not possibly stop this nightmare. Because Rwanda's problems were spiritual, the victory would never come except through spiritual warfare. The Lord showed us that through prayer we were to attack this army of demons slaughtering the Rwandans.

Again, the antenna on one of our big Voice of Hope stations in the Middle East was turned directly toward Rwanda and we commenced broadcasting God's omnipotent Word at these murdering spirits. We bound and cast out demons night and day and prayed for a loosing of the people.

Within weeks, the slaughter of the Rwandans slackened. To God be the glory! It has again become possible to distribute food and medicine to the needy. Now we broadcast evangelism, teaching, and healing to these precious people.

Can spiritual warfare blunt satanic attacks on our country too? The Lord asks, "Is there anything too hard for Me?" You know, there are two big and powerful weapons to win this victory: intercessory prayer and spiritual warfare. A brief word again on each of these might be helpful.

Intercessory Prayer

Intercessory prayer experienced a dramatic rebirthing some years back, and prayer groups have changed the course of recent spiritual history. The combined ministry of the prayer warriors has birthed 100,000 new churches and revivals in 100 countries. Prayer really works!

The day that we Christians quit wringing our hands over the woes of the world and start lifting up our problems to God, victories will burst forth. Already millions of people have been saved and thousands healed. In most intercessory prayers, we fervently speak to God about our personal needs, our church, loved ones, finances, and friends. This has pleased God and has brought results.

Spiritual Warfare

More recently there has been a restoration of spiritual warfare, perhaps God's most powerful strategy of all. He has backed you and me through the Holy Spirit, to engage the devil wherever he strikes. Jesus said, "...Go ye into all the world, and preach the gospel.... And these signs shall follow them that believe; *In My name shall they cast out devils...*" (Mk. 16:15,17).

When we battle in spiritual warfare, the Lord tells us first to put on the whole armor of God (see Eph. 6:10-17). As spiritual warriors, we then attack the devil's kingdom as it is affecting life here on earth. When we minister in this dimension, we declare directly to these wicked spirits in the power and authority of Jesus and the Word of God. The Holy Spirit's power is then activated through us for victory. In intercessory prayer we speak to God. In spiritual warfare we directly confront and command the evil spirits in Jesus' name and with the full authority of God's Word.

Reaching the World

Vital leaders and churches are now working to bring a full restoration of this spiritual power strategy over the enemy. Some of the leaders of this movement are Dr. Peter Wagner, Cindy Jacobs, Intercessors For America, Dr. Derek Prince, George Otis, Jr., Dean Sherman, Jack Hayford, and Ed Cole.

We asked these outstanding leaders to make spiritual warfare broadcasts over our world network against the forces of darkness in Washington, in the rest of our country, and in the world's trouble spots. What a potent army this is!

National and regional elections immediately following the Voice of Hope warfare campaign against corruption and wickedness in the land were startling. The biggest overthrow in recent memory of entrenched politicians took place. A new pursuit for national righteousness and a turning back to God burst forth.

The authority of Heaven is wanting to fully back you and me. Because of this you can bring more power to bear on the healing of our country than the president himself!

Our nations are now perched on a demon-driven volcano, ready to erupt. The foundations of the nations are webbed with cracks. If we don't act, America could fall into history's graveyard of dead empires. Someone recently said, "There is a power so strong, it causes the ruler of this world to tremble!" That power is spiritual warfare in Jesus' name. Will you stand up with me and march for God?

Prayer is our atomic arsenal. Prayer is our invincible arsenal. "If My people, which are called by My name, shall humble themselves, and pray, and seek My face, and turn from their wicked ways; then will I hear from heaven, and will forgive their sin, and will heal their land" (2 Chron. 7:14).

Our lands have a terminal sickness because our national leaderships have turned their backs on God and gone whoring after humanism. This tragedy has been inspired by the devil himself. But God has given to you and me this potent new weapon, spiritual warfare, to fight down this evil assault on our nation and every other nation on earth.

Shout It From the Housetops

We recently decided we were to hold a month-long Cuban spiritual warfare campaign. It would involve intensive spiritual warfare, a call to salvation and healings. When our High Adventure team went to pray and to observe, it was deeply gratifying. Upon landing in Havana, they saw a large group of Cuban policemen. Seven of the policemen were listening to radios tuned to the Voice of Hope!

The Cubans described our daily broadcasts as raising up a flame, and said that this radio crusade acted like a torch that had set off a huge spiritual fire across the island. Some of the Castro guards stationed outside the churches listened to the preaching and broadcasts. Some stood unashamedly crying as they received the Lord. On one night of the new revival, 170 Cubans gave their hearts to Jesus at one small church.

We broadcast about this exciting visitation of God over our radio station. People then began to make their way toward the churches from back in the jungles and countryside. Some walked 150 miles, and they thronged the meetings. Church windows were opened so hundreds standing outside could hear. Many in witchcraft and in the African Sanataria religion were set free by listening to the spiritual warfare ministry.

One of our own staff members, Cipriano, told how a talking demon said, "You are standing in the cave of hell." Cipriano was ministering in an occult region in Havana, and he knew this was accurate. Four demons were cast out of people over the next half hour. One 19-year-old girl was oppressed with a spirit of suicide; that's all she could think about. All she wanted to do was to end her life. That evil spirit of destruction was cast out of her forever.

A husband and wife who lived 20 miles outside Havana had a terrible crisis. She had acute infection in her kidneys. The pain seemed beyond her ability to remain conscious, and they thought she was going to die. The nearest medical clinic was in Havana. Her husband made a bold decision and dragged her to his bicycle.

They commenced the long 20-mile bicycle ride on dirt roads to save her life. On the way out of their house she grabbed a High Adventure radio hoping to block out the thought of the terrible pain during the bumpy trip. They finally reached the halfway marker on the desperate journey. God's Word, pouring out of her little radio suddenly healed her completely!

In a big Havana prison an inmate had been given a High Adventure radio. Listening to it during the nights he was wonderfully saved, but while the prisoners were having lunch, another prisoner stole his radio. He was crestfallen. Some three weeks later that prisoner came back, handed him back his radio, and asked forgiveness. He told how he had been listening and had received Jesus.

The Air Is Alive

Prayers and spiritual warfare are also tremendously effective through the airwaves, and why not? Satan and his demonic beings have their abode above us. Satan's name is the prince of the power of the air. As God's Word is broadcast over powerful transmitters, it races into their domain at an awesome 186,000 miles per second.

The Word has a paralyzing and binding effect upon the enemy, setting captives free and healing the sick. Today we are experiencing a flow of heartpounding testimonies from listeners in 170 nations. Here are a few recent letter excerpts:

"My mother was confined to a mental ward near Havana for nineteen years. This has been agony to me, but I started listening to your station broadcasting prayers and spiritual warfare. Suddenly I received Jesus! My whole life changed. I got an idea for my mother and took my little radio and put it under her bed. In about two weeks the evil spirits fled out of her and she is home and joyful again!"—**Havana, Cuba**

"I went to the hospital to give birth to our third child, while my husband stayed with the other children. When the doctor brought my new baby, he told me she would not live but a few hours. He had taken x-rays to discover that she only had half a heart. She was blue and gasping for breath. I carried her home and when I walked in the door, the Voice of Hope was turned on and a man was binding the devil and praying for those who had severe physical problems. I ran to stand by the radio. My child started to breathe evenly and her color changed. Later that day the doctor's new x-rays showed she had received a brand new heart."—**Lebanon**

"To my favorite, best station, The Voice of Hope. I write these few lines to tell you how much I love and admire your radio station. I ask God for you to be in good health."—**Baghdad, Iraq**

"I have been receiving you loud and clear every day. I love the Word of God because it speaks to me anew every time I hear it. I don't ever miss the program, 'Today with Derek Prince.' I am being fed spiritually through your broadcasts. May God continue to bless and prosper your ministry."—**Tarkawa, Ghana**

"I suffered from an illness in my hip; the pain was so intense that I had to walk crooked. Through your spiritual warfare prayers, I was suddenly healed! Not only from my hip, but also from a tumor above one of my ears! I give God the glory and thank Him for your station."—**Coxcatlan, Mexico**

"I want to tell you about this radio station called the Voice of Hope. We thank the Lord, for it is such a help to our church in China. I personally listen to only one station and that is yours, the one we call the 'Holy Ghost Station.' Churches in China now feel very much that they need the power of the Holy Spirit, and now over the radio waves this truth is coming to us and is breaking down opposition in China. Now my spirit is on fire!"—**Beijing, China**

"My whole family listens to your programs. We love the Jesus songs. You are the only station that is heard here. May God bless you in this mighty work you do."—**Belarus, Russia**

"I listen to the programs with great interest over your station 'Wings of Hope.' I have come to Christ because of your Russian programs."—**Kazakhstan, Russia**

"When I am at sea on the big freighter, I can still hear the Gospel through your station. It is marvelous being able to take in the Word at sea."—**Skarhhahn, Sweden**

"I was very glad when I found the Voice of Hope, as if I found a precious treasure. You are like the voice of John the Baptist, leading us toward a better world. God can use His Word to change everyone who listens. I am Egyptian but work now in Jordan."—**Jordan**

"I am a regular listener who came to the Lord in 1986 after a Hindu background. I am Indian but now serve in the Saudi Coast Guard. Your broadcasts are blessings to me, helping me to grow in the Lord and give me adequate strength to prepare for Jesus' second coming. We have a small group here who listen and pray for one another."—**Saudi Arabia**

"I am so happy to let you know that High Adventure radio has become such a great blessing. Through listening all my family has accepted Christ as their Savior. My husband was an alcoholic and now all he wants to do is be in church."—**Guatemala**

"Dear High Adventure, I would like you to know that your broadcasts have richly blessed me. I am twenty-five years old. I am now baptized and know Jesus is my only Savior. Thank you for your radio stations."—**Damascus, Syria**

"I am thankful for the Voice of Hope, which brought me salvation through Jesus and the Holy Spirit. Now I pray for sick people in hospitals and God heals many. Thank you."—**Alexandria, Egypt**

"I got hold of a radio here in the prison and started listening to your station. After about a month I gave my life to Jesus. Now thirty other prisoners have also become Christians."—**Chile**

Chapter 5

Fighting the Good Fight

"No weapon that is formed against thee shall prosper..." (Is. 54:17). "Fight the good fight of faith" (1 Tim. 6:12a). "...endure hardness, as a good soldier of Jesus Christ" (2 Tim. 2:3).

We are engaged in a war—whether we like it or not. Don't be deceived. The New Testament refers to this war as "our warfare." But who are we fighting? Certainly not human beings and governments, but spiritual wickedness in high places and our adversary, satan, who seeks to devour and destroy us (see 1 Pet. 5:8).

In Paul's great battle letter to the Ephesians, he outlines a hierarchy of demonic beings who are our spiritual enemies and says, "For we wrestle not against flesh and blood, but against principalities, against powers, against the rulers of the darkness of this world, against spiritual wickedness in high places" (Eph. 6:12).

Therefore, while we are in this world, we need to put on the *full armor* of God, not just a leisure suit, because the armor of God protects us from demonic onslaught. Satan is a formidable enemy, and yet, this enemy is also a defeated foe through the death and resurrection of Christ. These same principalities and powers identified in Ephesians 6 are also called defeated foes in Colossians 2:15: "...having [disarmed] principalities and powers, He made a [public spectacle] of them...triumphing over them in it."

Show and Tell

The custom of ancient victors was to humiliate a conquered king and army by parading him around, stripped of his weapons, armor, and clothes. Likewise, Jesus descended into hell, conquered satan and his cohorts, openly paraded them in the spirit world before God and the heavenly beings, and made a universal "show and tell" of them—demonstrating that they had been defeated for all of eternity. Jesus now holds the keys of hell and death (see Rev. 1:18). The sentence of doom has been passed, and satan knows his time is short before he will be cast into the lake of fire.

In the meantime, satan and his vast hierarchy of fallen angels (one-third of the heavenly hosts) are waging a guerrilla warfare against the Kingdom of God. It is our job as soldiers of Jesus Christ to enforce the Lord's victory. This enforcing and occupying is what the Lord meant when He said, "And from the days of John the Baptist until now the kingdom of heaven suffereth violence, and the violent [that is us] take it by force" (Mt. 11:12).

Violence against whom? People? No, never! Demons? Yes! This verse is what spiritual warfare is all about. It also speaks of the believers' zeal and ardor.

If you don't believe there's a spiritual war going on, just try to reclaim some territory lost by the Church to the powers of darkness—like prayer in the schools, abortion, pornography, and homosexuality. You will soon learn that spiritual weapons are absolutely necessary in order to survive.

But what are some of those spiritual weapons? Here are some powerful truths for your own spiritual warfare. These are weapons that the warrior Paul says are not carnal but are terribly mighty (see 2 Cor. 10:4).

> The name of Jesus—"...In My name shall they cast out devils..." (Mk. 16:17).

> The blood of Jesus and the words of our testimonies—"And they overcame him by the blood of the Lamb, and by the [utterance] of their testimony..." (Rev. 12:11).

> Binding and loosing—"And I will give unto thee the keys of the kingdom of heaven: and whatsoever thou shalt bind on earth shall be bound in heaven: and whatsoever thou shalt loose on earth shall be loosed in heaven" (Mt. 16:19).

> The full armor of God—"That ye may be able to stand [in the evil day]" (see Eph. 6:11,13).

> Angels of the Lord—"encamps around those who fear Him, and He delivers them" (Ps. 34:7b NIV).

> The gifts of the Spirit—(see 1 Cor. 12). These are mighty weapons that build the Church, break yokes, and help to destroy the kingdom of darkness whenever they are

applied. Paul says we are to "war a good warfare [with prophecies]" (1 Tim. 1:18b).

Our "[faith] that overcomes the world"— (1 Jn. 5:4b). Never forget that faith is one of our big guns.

Jesus, the Lord of hosts, needs the Body of Christ to become more militant through spiritual warfare. The mood of the Spirit is for intensive spiritual warfare in this generation. Why? Satan has increased his attacks on the people and work of God. Our children are at risk more than ever. So much garbage is thrown at them that it takes a major sifting out of their minds every day with the washing of the Word.

The minds of adults are also increasingly under attack. Ask any believer who has even a morsel of discernment; they will tell you that our enemy seems to be more subtle, cunning, and vicious in his ambushments. This is because satan knows that his time is very, very short. He is madly kicking up the dust in ruthless, desperate attempts to touch the throne of God. He knows, of course, that he can't do that. He failed to unseat God, but he can nevertheless touch the throne by proxy every time he causes one of God's children to fall or to sin. Giving place to satan in our lives brings reproach in some way to the crown, to the throne, and to the King of kings.

We need to wake up out of what is almost a spiritual stupor. We must stop the enemy from making further inroads into our lives and into the Church. A lot of people talk about spiritual warfare, but not enough practice it.

I asked one of the leading authorities on spiritual warfare to do a spiritual warfare broadcast over the Voice of

Hope Network against the powers and principalities that were wreaking havoc in Rwanda. But when I returned to his office to pick up his message, he had not made the broadcast. He was honest enough to admit that he could teach the theory of spiritual warfare but, in fact, he did not know how to do it. This general in the Body of Christ simply admitted, "I don't know how to put it into practice."

We want to teach you not only *how*, but *why*, spiritual warfare is necessary to survive this generation. We need to fire the Guns of God, which is just a way of saying, "We need to wield the sword of the Spirit!"

The term *spiritual warfare* scares some people because they are afraid of the devil. They wonder if it is scriptural to engage demons and to fight using the Word of God as a weapon. We sometimes forget Scriptures like First Timothy 6:12a: "Fight the good fight of faith" and Ephesians 6:12: "For we wrestle...against spiritual [hosts of] wickedness in [the heavenly] places."

A Nighttime Visit From the Devil

Remember now, we should never be afraid of the devil. Satan's Waterloo was at Calvary. The Body of Christ would make great strides if we understood satan like the great apostle Smith Wigglesworth of England did. He really knew the devil's lack of power and authority over blood-washed believers. One night Wigglesworth was sleeping in a creepy old house where he was a guest. The wind was howling outside and causing the shutters to beat against the windows. There was thunder and lightning. Suddenly, Wigglesworth was awakened by the racket and saw, standing at the foot of his bed, the devil himself.

"Oh, it's just you," Wigglesworth said, and he turned over and went back to sleep!

Wigglesworth was so secure in Jesus by faith that he didn't even bother to tell the devil to leave. The devil left because his pride couldn't stand the presence of that kind of faith in Almighty God.

Mighty Warrior

"The Lord is a man of war: the Lord is His name" (Ex. 15:3). The Bible is militant. Somehow Jesus has been classified as a pacifist because He came as the Lamb of God. When He returns, sinners will cry out, "Rocks, fall on me! The wrath of the Lamb has come." Jesus wielded a whip in the temple area, and at His return He comes with the armies of Heaven as a Man of War, wearing a vesture dipped in blood (see Rev. 19:13). God the Father is also described in many places in the Bible as a Warrior, make no mistake about that! We see the lightning of His sword. Joshua spoke to the "Commander of the army of the Lord" (see Josh. 5:14-15 NIV).

If satan was defeated at the cross, why is spiritual warfare necessary? Satan is defeated but is still on the loose and allowed to try the hearts of men. He has no legal right to harass you unless you give place to him. Jesus expects us to use the spiritual authority He bequeathed to us to bind these demonic beings.

What have you bound this week? What have you loosed? If none, you are not walking in your authority. Spiritual warfare is not an option; it is a New Testament command to bind devils, to resist devils, and to cast out devils.

"But," you say, "I can't talk to devils." When we do spiritual warfare, it is important that we not be drawn into any two-way conversations with spirits. Don't ask them any questions. They love that, but remember that they lie and lie and lie. This can intrigue and distract our spiritual tasks at hand. But you have every right and authority to command devils to leave. So just speak out the worship to God, the truth of the Word, and the fact that satan and his demons are already defeated. Declare them to be bound and order them to cease their evil work—a one-way communication only.

Casting out devils is a sign that is to follow every believer, not just those in the fivefold ministry of apostle, prophet, evangelist, teacher, and pastor. Look what the Great Commission in Mark 16:17 says: "And these signs shall follow them that believe; In My name shall they cast out [demons]...."

Casting out devils by commanding them to leave should be as common and ordinary to every believer as taking out the garbage. If you find that strife has broken out in your home, don't tolerate it. Perceive that the devil may be behind the scenes. Go to the door and say, "Out, devil, in Jesus' name. In faith I strike the doorpost with the blood of Jesus, and you are trespassing!" You will be amazed at the peace that will return to your home as the devil flees!

Jesus spoke to devils and commanded them to leave. They did, and He is our example. The apostle Paul routinely commanded devils to leave.

You defeat the devil, who is seeking your destruction, by using the specific Word of God that applies to your situation. That is why you *must* know the Word of God. There is an index at the end of this book with verses correlating to many personal problems. These will be helpful to you in choosing appropriate Scriptures when you are attacked by the enemy.

Change the atmosphere in which you live by sending forth the Word like bullets out of your mouth to target any mountain or problem that arises to defeat you. Those bullets of the Word of God will shatter any demonic foe as you speak the Word of God to it in faith.

We should not speak things to the devil that are not in the Word of God. That is both careless and witless because our own words are not powerful. But God's Word is guaranteed to be quick, powerful, and sharper than any two-edged sword (see Heb. 4:12). Do you see the difference?

A major principle of war is: Never underestimate your enemy. That is why in Jude the archangel Michael when disputing with the devil for the body of Moses did not presume to bring against him a personal, railing accusation, but instead said, "The Lord rebuke you!" (see Jude 9)

As long as we are proclaiming the Word of God and our lives are kept under the blood of Jesus, we are on safe ground. As the old hymn says, "I stay right under the blood, where the devil can do me no harm!"

Another term for spiritual warfare, which may be more palatable to some people, is "the ministry of the proclamation of the Word." But we are not wrestling with flesh and blood; we have to use spiritual weapons, and the Word is the weapon that causes the devil to flee.

He sent His word, and healed them, and delivered them from their destructions (Psalm 107:20).

For as the rain cometh down, and the snow from heaven, and...watereth the earth, and maketh it bring forth and bud, that it may give seed to the sower, and bread to the eater: so shall My word be that goeth forth out of My mouth: it shall not return unto Me void, but it shall accomplish that which I please [and purpose], and it shall prosper in the thing whereto I sent it (Isaiah 55:10-11).

Let us get a mental picture of how the Word works when it is sent. Psalm 107 says that when God sends His Word its decree has the power to heal and to deliver people from their destructions. The Word, when spoken, cannot be seen by our eyes as it travels through the earth, but it does travel. Just like light or radio beams, it travels.

The Word keeps moving until, like an arrow of deliverance, it hits the target for which it has been sent. Distance is no problem in the spirit world. Not only is the Word sent, but in Isaiah 55, we see that the Word returns. It goes full circle. It does the job, it prospers, and then it returns like a boomerang! But, unlike a boomerang, the Word does not return empty. Isn't that absolutely marvelous? It cannot return void, but accomplishes the purpose for which it has been sent. The Word has a big return!

We are co-laborers with God when we use our authority and decree the Word into situations. "Thou shalt also decree a thing, and it shall be established unto thee: and the light shall shine upon thy ways" (Job 22:28).

Broadcasting From Your Prayer Closet

We can send the Word to any individual or nation. We can use our prayer transmitter to carry the spoken Word, but we can also broadcast from our prayer closet. How? God backs His Word and sends it forth through the atmosphere as we speak it in faith. Isn't that awesome to contemplate?

So where there is darkness, we proclaim the Word of the Lord, which is the will of the Lord as revealed in the Holy Bible. The Word, when it is sent forth in the power of the Holy Ghost, cannot return empty, but accomplishes what He purposes.

Specific Ammunition

In every situation that seems oppressive, we should ask the Lord for our specific ammunition: "Lord, speak to me from your Word; give me light in this situation." Always, graciously, He will supply a *rhema* (enlightened) verse or verses that will be the right weapon whereby you will succeed.

If you are having trouble with your children, seek the Lord for a verse, such as, "And all thy children shall be taught of the Lord; and great shall be the peace of thy children" (Is. 54:13). What is the return on that Word when it is sent? Peace—for you and your children.

If you're having trouble with your marriage or job, ask God for the ammunition from His Word, and then speak that Word as a salvo into the situation. Next, add patience to your faith. Wait for the Word to do its work! Remember, it is not even *possible* for that Word to return void.

We each know people or families who have had persistent problems in health, alcoholism, depression, chronic financial struggles, violence, or mental recurrences. In ministering to such people, I sometimes learn that their own pattern of woes are similar to those of their parents and grandparents. Friends will say, "It runs in their family." But the Bible tells us that curses that are put upon people are sometimes carried through the family for three or four generations.

Modern medical specialists may diagnose these phenomena as genetic. The psychologists often say they have been inherited from the individuals' parents. The exciting thing I have experienced is that these can often be healed and broken through spiritually attacking the evil spirit that has come through some curse from the past.

There is such an increase today of witchcraft, satan worship, and the occult that it isn't surprising that, at some place, we too may have been the target of such a demonic attack. May I suggest that you pray, along with several other strong Christians, to break the hold of any curse or demonic attack that has been laid upon you. Don't forget—you could have picked up a life-troubling problem even by going many years ago to a fortune teller, a seance, or the like. Deal with this speedily and watch your life begin to change for the better.

Maria was saved at the age of 17 having come to America with her family before she was old enough to start school. She had no memory of her earliest years in a foreign land, nor of the fact that witchcraft and occultic practices were common there.

As Maria grew in the things of the Lord, she met a dedicated Christian man and they were married. Together they agreed to serve Jesus in whatever way He called them. It seemed they were doing all the right things to experience success in their spiritual life, and yet they and their children were plagued with unexplained disasters—car accidents, a house fire, illness, and financial setbacks. It seemed that no matter how much they prayed nothing changed.

And then they heard a powerful teaching on the need to break generational curses. The more they listened, the more they wondered if this might be the source of their problems. Maria's husband was from a long line of Christians and knew his family history well. They were sure the problems didn't originate there.

They sat down and talked with Maria's family, and after some "digging," they discovered that Maria's great-grandmother had been involved in witchcraft. And so they attacked the problem at its root, renouncing past spiritual ties and binding the enemy's continued working in their family. The change was immediate! There is now a peace and prosperity in their home that they had never experienced before.

If Maria's situation sounds like something you've been experiencing, pray and seek God as to its source. Then, once you've identified that source, just speak to any evil spirit who has been oppressing your life. Proclaim forcefully, "In the authority of Jesus' name and God's Word, I break this curse forever. I bind you, evil spirit, and cast you out!" Now ask God to fill the vacuum that is left with a new love for the Lord and to shut the door forever to this evil spirit.

Don't always expect a snap five minutes of spiritual war against any kind of spirit to do the job. Jesus said that some of those spirits come out only after prayer and fasting.

If Michael the mighty archangel had to do spiritual warfare against the prince of Persia spirit, we too should be prepared to be persevering spiritual pitbulls until we achieve total victory.

Bandit Bound by the Word

There was a Norwegian missionary to China who knew these principles before spiritual warfare became topical.

Her ship was captured by bandits for more than three weeks' time. They threatened to steal all of her property and to kill her with a pistol. As one of the bandits said he would shoot unless she handed over her goods, she said, "You cannot kill me without God's permission because it is written in the Bible that no weapon formed against me shall prosper."

Many times the bandit threatened to shoot her, but always she bound that demon of murder with the Word, "No weapon formed against me shall prosper." The bandit seemed powerless to pull the trigger day after day. One of the bandits said sarcastically and repeatedly to the other bandits, "She says we cannot shoot her because her Bible says that no weapon formed against her shall prosper." But even in his sarcasm he was quoting the Word of God! She was never once harmed.

Chapter 6

From Theory to Action

It was 11:22 on Monday morning when the phone rang bringing a terrifying announcement. A little two-year-old girl named Jenna had drowned in the swimming pool. I remember throwing a tablet I was working on into the air and then, like a blur, racing for the car.

I had been working on this very book dealing with spiritual warfare and had been heavily engaged in spiritual combat with the forces of darkness here at the edge of time. The thought flashed through my mind, *The drowning of this precious little girl is a vicious attack from the adversary! We must not give him a victory over little Jenna.*

Upon arrival at the house with the swimming pool, we saw that the street was filled with fire trucks, a rescue van, police cars, and an ambulance. Little two-year-old Jenna had been discovered at the bottom of the pool where she had lain for 10 or 15 minutes. Jenna's mother dove into the pool, brought the child up, and laid her on the kitchen table. Her skin was blue, contrasting with her very blond hair. Jenna was lifeless.

Her mom commenced strenuous artificial respiration while her father and the rest of us cried out in passionate prayer. Water and vomit were brought up from Jenna's lungs by her mother's swift work, and then the experts stepped in and raced her by ambulance to a hospital. There in the intensive care ward they hooked her up to a respirator, oxygen, and dripping medication.

Still no sign of life. Jenna was in a deep, deep coma. By all visible signs, she was gone. Those on the hospital staff warned that the situation was not very hopeful, because she had lain at the bottom of the pool for so long.

The hours stretched on through the night as the family gathered in the waiting room. From time to time one would slip in to look at the beautiful little girl, and the tears would well up. The hospital staff said that these kinds of cases frequently end in death, pneumonia, brain damage, or crippling—not a very optimistic prognosis.

But we would not give in. We unholstered our prayer guns repeatedly. With one gun we cried out with passion to the Father for His mercy and His miracle. With our other prayer gun we undertook very intensive and fierce spiritual warfare directly against the adversary using God's Word.

The hours ticked on. The father and mother never left the hospital even though there was nothing tangible they could do. Finally, my wife and I insisted that the parents slip out for a couple of hours to a restaurant in honor of Jenna's mom's birthday that fell on the day after the tragic accident.

I volunteered to sit in the room with Jenna while they were gone. About an hour later, the nurse who was in the room with us suddenly shouted for me to look at Jenna. She pointed out how first one eyelid and then the other were flickering about a quarter open.

The nurse said, "Could it be? This is the way it looks when someone comes back from death. Jenna can't speak to you because of the tubes in her throat, but ask her a question that requires a yes answer, then one that requires a no answer. We need to learn if her brain is starting to work again."

I commenced by asking, "Jenna, how would you like to go home to your grandma's house and play with Amber?" (Amber is a shaggy golden retriever with whom Jenna loves to romp.) Suddenly Jenna opened her eyes all the way and looked at me, then nodded her head up and down.

Delighted, I continued. "Jenna, how would you like to go and play with Turbo?" (Turbo is a frisky cat, whom Jenna doesn't like at all.) Again she opened her eyes, but this time she shook her head no. Tears welled up in our eyes.

After several minutes of this kind of interrogation, I got very close to Jenna's ear and asked her a special question, "Jenna, where have you been? Did you visit Heaven?" Now her eyes flew wide open as she turned her little head toward me and vigorously nodded it up and down.

Finally I asked, "Jenna, did you see Jesus while you were there?" Still looking at me with that gaze I shall never forget, she again nodded her head decisively up and down.

The nurse seemed both impressed and dumbfounded. Little Jenna was released from the hospital two days later with no evidence of her near-death experience. Just following her release from the hospital, a young woman from Washington state who knew Jenna and the family sent a FAX. In it she told how she had experienced a dream during the time Jenna was in the coma. In the dream, which she described as extremely vivid, she saw little Jenna sitting on Jesus' lap in Heaven.

Truly this was a resurrection! I shall never cease wondering about the power and practicality of prayer. In this case, spiritual warfare and intercessory prayer had raised one from the dead, but it also brings victory in the less dramatic crises of our lives.

We must understand that using the Guns of God works for all of God's people whether we are fighting for nations or for loved ones in our own family. It's time to stop being spectators. We shouldn't sing "Onward Christian Soldiers" if we are going to act like spiritual wimps! Our own Lord isn't called God Almighty for nothing.

In another instance, a friend whose father was rushed to the hospital emergency room with a heart attack was asked if she needed her pastor to come to the hospital to pray.

Her answer? "Don't bother my pastor. He's done his job. He taught *me* how to pray and how to do spiritual warfare." She took authority over the sudden physical attack on her dad and prayed the prayer of faith to raise him up. He was healed!

You see, our pastors may not always be available, so we too must learn to intercede on behalf of our families, our cities, our nations, and our problems. But should you get involved in spiritual warfare? Yes, God is *commanding* you to resist the devil so that he will flee (see Jas. 4:7).

Have you read the book *The Intercessor* about Rees Howells? His intercessory prayer ministry helped to turn the tide during World War II. Many want to emulate his intense yet sometimes strange prayer life because it got results.

It is important to grasp that all believers are called to pray. In fact, we are told to "pray without ceasing" (1 Thess. 5:17). There's no profit in prayerlessness. We all must become active in spiritual warfare or pay the consequences of satan's wiles.

Some believers have an anointing to lead a prayer group or to be an intercessor to carry the burden of the Lord, to birth the unseen into the seen. There are also prayer warriors among us who have a great fighting spirit. By faith they reach up and bring down to earth what's already been accomplished in Heaven.

God is watching for intercessors! "And He saw that there was no man, and wondered that there was no intercessor" (Is. 59:16a).

Touching God on Behalf of Others

Intercession is great and unbiased. It is not self-centered. Intercession stands in the gap on behalf of others to plead their case before God like a spiritual attorney. Andrew Murray described intercession as "asking and receiving heavenly gifts to carry to men." Catherine Marshall defines intercession as "touching God on behalf of others."

Violent Encounters

But there is also a violent, stronger side to intercession. When the word *intercession* appears in the Old Testament, it is often the translation of the Hebrew word *paga*, which means a "violent encounter"—like the wrestling that Paul referred to in Ephesians 6, commonly known as the "warfare chapter."

Examples of "survivors" from intercession in the Bible are Jacob, who wrestled with the angel all night, and Moses whose pleadings averted God from destroying Israel. Abraham interceded on behalf of the people of Sodom and Gomorrah. He had already "bargained with God" to save that wicked place if even 50 righteous could be found, then 45, then 40, then 30, then 20, but he stopped at 10. However, God gave no indication that his intercession should have stopped at the number 10! (See Genesis 18:16-33.)

Moses was willing to put his life on the line when he interceded on behalf of Israel. He offered God his own life to make atonement on Sinai for Israel. In the same spirit, the apostle Paul was willing to be accursed if it meant that Israel could be saved. This is the true spirit of intercession. We must not take it lightly.

In Joshua's experience as an intercessor, he came to the heart of the matter in moving God. He asked, "What will You do for Your great name?" (see Josh. 7:9) The intercessor pleads to avert judgment and to save souls because God's eternal purposes and great name are at stake. In other words, intercession asks God, "Are You going to let the devil cloud Your reputation in this matter? What will You do on behalf of Your awesome name? What about all of Your earlier promises? Shall not the Judge of all the earth do right?" That is heavy!

So intercession is usually associated with strong, aggressive prayer to God.

A Ministry of Declaration

On the other hand, spiritual warfare is a ministry of declaration, or proclamation, of the Word as well as wonderful high praises to God. All of this wreaks havoc and confusion in the kingdom of darkness as well as accomplishing binding and loosing. When we participated in the great gospel campaigns in Africa, spiritual warfare was a big ingredient.

The local intercessors, upon being questioned, could identify the major spirits that were hindrances, and mighty swirls of prayer of binding and loosing were a major part of setting the captives free. The evangelism harvest was totally dependent upon binding the spirits ahead of time.

Spiritual warfare is not prayer to God. It is Word warfare against an enemy who is a spiritual being: "For our struggle is not against flesh and blood, but against the rulers, against the authorities, against the powers of this dark world and against the spiritual forces of evil in the heavenly realms" (Eph. 6:12 NIV). Because our enemy is a spirit, our weapons must correspondingly be spiritual: "For the weapons of our warfare are not [physical], but [they are] mighty through God to the pulling down of strong holds" (2 Cor. 10:4).

Word Wars

In spiritual warfare, what are the Guns of God? *Words!* Yes, we are engaged in a word war, and God's Word is what we fight with to utterly outgun our enemy.

Never be over-awed by our adversary. The Bible even tells us what we will say when we finally see him. We won't be impressed one bit and will exclaim, "Is this the man that caused the world to tremble?" (see Is. 14:16)

The battle is for the souls of men, and our guns are His words! The Bible describes God's words as weapons. The devil also uses words for his weapons. But his words are lies, fiery darts, and deadly arrows that are aimed as an ambush. He is a liar and the father of lies.

The results of power unleashed through God's Word can be seen in spiritual history. Here is an example. The Lord instructed the children of God how to fashion the Ark and then told them to place within it the stone tablets, which are the foundation of God's Word to us. The laws were written on Sinai by the finger of God Himself.

This "shrine of the Book" was always to go before them. When a battle broke out the Ark was to go before the army of the Israelites. The power of God that was unleashed brought victory—but not at Ai (see Josh. 7–8). Therein is a powerful message to us today. Knowing the reason for their defeat can insure our own victory in spiritual warfare. You see, God's Word, the tablets of stone, were also to be accompanied by righteousness.

After the terrible Ai defeat, Joshua found that Achan had secretly stolen an evil heathen idol. This offended God and diminished His power of the Ark. Achan's sins were finally dealt with. Then, when the Israelite army headed by the holy Ark came back to Ai, a glorious victory was won.

So we should cleanse ourselves through confession and prayer and ask God's forgiveness for our sins before we engage in spiritual warfare. The results will be like night and day. It is written, "...Seek ye first the kingdom of God, *and His* righteousness; and all these things shall be added unto you" (Mt. 6:33); and "The fear of the Lord is the beginning of wisdom" (Prov. 9:10a).

Turn Your Radio On

It would be natural if you were to think, *How can you expect results when you do spiritual warfare by radio broadcasting?* Think of this: people are saved and healed, and spirits are bound regularly in our church services. To accomplish this spiritual harvest, the pastor speaks through a microphone to the congregation, and it produces important spiritual results.

Broadcasting through a microphone carries God's Word at the speed of 186,000 miles per second. Three of our Voice of Hope stations operate at six million watts (erp), and the Word can be heard 3,000 to 6,000 miles away.

Satan's domain is in the skies. He is called the prince of the power of the air. Little wonder that his forces are terribly affected and weakened by a continuous bombardment of the Word. It is not surprising that we receive thousands of testimonies from listeners who have been saved, healed, and delivered through broadcasting.

If the Word in stone, carried in a box (the Holy Ark), won battles for the army of the Israelites, then shouting His glorious Word throughout the earth also brings trouble to our enemy and divine help to the listeners.

Chain Reaction Ignited

An American missionary in Bulgaria has been involved in great spiritual warfare over that Balkan nation, that has been torn by Communism and is in the grip of many religious spirits coming both from the East and the West. Cliff McCorkle wrote to his fellow spiritual warriors: "What a glorious campaign! We direct God's Words like spiritual arrows across a nation, and we make known the ways of God. When we make this known to the rulers and the prince of the power of the air, miracles take place!"

An astounding chain reaction of spiritual responses is ignited. First, the truth produces new faith and peace in the hearts of the unsaved. The same words have an incredible explosive effect against the lies of darkness. The truth announced boldly in faith goes forth like an eruption of laser light shattering the darkness and creating fear, division, and panic within satan's army! Those same words bless our heavenly Father and His worthy Son who listen to our every word spoken.

Spiritual warfare is bold to speak the gospel in the midst of opposition. The name of Jesus is the most powerful name in the universe, and He gave us the right to use that name like His power-of-attorney. We have been given the Holy Spirit to teach us how to wield the name of Jesus. The Book of Acts is a record of the Church using the Word and the name of Jesus to shake the world.

To move from theory to practice, here are a few tips in learning to engage in spiritual warfare:

Develop a Holy Ghost Consciousness

A true spiritual warrior is more conscious of the presence of the Holy Ghost than of the demonic realm and territorial spirits. Reinhard Bonnke tells the story of a time he went to India and was met at the airport by a churchman who said in a hushed voice, "Reinhard, do you feel them? Do you feel their presence?"

"Feel whom?" Reinhard asked.

The churchman answered, "The demons, of course!"

Reinhard's blue eyes flashed in tandem with his bold retort, "No, I am far more aware of the Holy Spirit than any demons."

That is the mentality of a true warrior! The spiritual warrior knows his Supreme Commander, and his morale is never undermined in the haunts of devils.

But a good warrior needs weapons and knowledge of how to use them. The more of God's Word you know, the more power you have at your disposal. The Word floats up out of your spirit, and the Holy Spirit brings them to remembrance at just the right moment. "Let the word of Christ dwell in you richly in all wisdom" (Col. 3:16a).

Some intercessors have such a perpetual consciousness of the blood covering that they don't have to plead it constantly. This is because they know it and the demons know it, just as the spirit acknowledged in the sons of Sceva incident: "Jesus I know, and Paul I know; but who are ye?" (Acts 19:15b) But in most cases it is not only faith building but wise to declare before God and before the demonic world something like this:

> "We plead the blood of Jesus over ourselves, over this room and everybody in it, over our loved ones, possessions, and property. [And you know, there is a great truth in that old hymn, 'There is power, power, wonder working power in the precious blood of the Lamb.']

> "In the name of Jesus we take the sword of the Spirit to send forth His Word as a weapon into this problem. In the name of Jesus we bind the evil forces and loose the Spirit of Truth."

Then we continue as the Spirit leads us.

Declare the Word With Authority

This step separates the victors from the spectators. The next time you perceive the devil is behind something, don't just let him have his way. We tolerate the devil too much.

You are wearing the armor of God. Now take the sword of the Spirit and wield it with your mouth. As the Guns of God send forth the truth of God's Word into that dark situation, they will shatter the enemy's lies and his strength, and they will accomplish the work of the Lord.

Always remember your authority and never back down. No matter how much noise the devil makes or dust he kicks up—having done all—stand! Look the devil in the eyes, and with the finger of God command him. In many African campaigns, dealing with all sorts of demonpossessed people, we learned the Bible truth that you can stay calm even in the face of a madman because "greater is He that is in you, than he that is in the world" (1 Jn. 4:4b).

Be confident as you remember how you are working with these mighty weapons and that you are of the light. The devil's realm is darkness. Remember that darkness cannot even stay where the light comes. Thus you are invincible when moving in God's ways and wielding His weapons. The power of light always drives out darkness.

Chapter 7

Keeping Our Spiritual Guns Blazing

It sends thrills through my being when I read, "Let there be light: and there was light" (Gen. 1:3b). As a child, when asked how God made the world and the stars, my little mind would visualize Him working with big tools and scaffolding. But His ways are above our ways; He just spoke the world and the universe into being. This is how powerful it is to speak out God's Word. It has never changed!

My mind recalls Jericho. This great walled city is the oldest city on earth. Its walls were so thick and strong that people were able to live in them. Rahab was one such Jericho "resident of the walls."

God had promised the million children of Israel, who were on their way back from Egypt, to lead them into the Promised Land. But they faced a big problem. The highly fortified city of Jericho with its huge walls was sprawled right in the path of God's chosen. They couldn't taste of God's promise unless Jericho, which was the gate to the Promised Land, was opened.

No tactic of the Jewish military could crack this impossible situation. Finally, God gave them a plan that seemed illogical. But fortunately they followed His Word and marched around the city for a number of days. At an appointed moment, the shofars were blown with abandonment.

The children of Israel shouted the name of God, and then the Lord instantly spoke to thousands of tons of stone and atomized the walls of Jericho. God holds all matter together by His Word, and in this dramatic moment, He commanded the walls to vaporize into nothingness.

I love to go to Jericho and see the archaeologists searching for the walls of Jericho. Ever since God created the moon, the stars, the sun, and the galaxies, they have remained with their lights ablaze. At God's Word Jericho's walls came tumbling down. The Israelites entered into the Promised Land stepping over the rubble of Jericho. This was powerful spiritual warfare.

Spiritual warfare has been given to the family of God, and with it we can prepare the way of the Lord here at the close of this age. God has armed us to put the devil on notice along with the fallen angels and the entire demonic army of satan. Using the might of God's Word and the power of the Holy Spirit, we should act upon its omnipotence and never-changing quality. We must use the spiritual weapons He has put into our hands.

Likewise, these weapons, when wielded by us in compliance with God's Word, create what I call the "footprints of God." During Jesus' most active earthly ministry along Galilee, most of His activity involved ministry to the hurting and the desperate. He healed the crippled, restored sight to the blind, opened the ears of the deaf, cleansed the lepers, raised the dead, cast out demons, and did uncounted miracles.

Those who saw these wonders knew that only God could accomplish such things. So they came by the thousands to see Him as the word spread to nations 'round about. At times, the crowds following Him numbered 20,000, for they perceived that He was speaking and acting under the power of God. His words and actions were a powerful magnet drawing the desperate into healing and into the family of the Lord.

But what can we do to follow in our Lord's footsteps, to continue His work here on earth? Plenty! We can take part in spiritual warfare personally. We have only one major enemy, and we can bind and loose those things that are destructive to our friends, our families, and our cities. The Lord says that whatever we bind on earth He will bind in Heaven and whatever we loose on earth in His name He will loose in Heaven. (See Matthew 16:19.) Remember Jesus said, "...I give unto you power...over all the power of the enemy" (Lk. 10:19a).

If we, in the name of Jesus, bind the demons and their evil workings, the Lord immediately partners with us to bring about the victory. Maybe you have been complaining for years about the evil that is rising in your schools, in the gangs, the criminality in your neighborhoods, drugs, pornography, homosexual and lesbian predators, and child molesters. Now you can wage spiritual warfare against these demonic strongholds and paralyze the evil spirits that inspire them.

Satan is called the prince of this world. In a sense we are "in his house." Little wonder things seem to be falling apart all around us here at the end of time. But God didn't put us here defenseless. He says we are to bind the strongman and his followers and spoil his house. We are destined to take away the things and the people he has stolen after we bind him, in Jesus' authority.

Remember, there is no merit in screaming, yelling, and calling satan names. In fact, Jesus asks us to say, "The Lord rebuke you, satan!" However, that doesn't apply to the evil spirit beings. Likewise, when we conduct spiritual warfare, we shouldn't speak it silently. Shout the Word! Don't forget, it was how the children of Israel shouted in response to God's directive that forced the walls of Jericho to come down.

The Guns of God may be turned against any demonic situation. You can speak the Word of God and take authority over these evil spirits. You can address them and repeat the Scriptures, which are listed in the index of this book for your use. Remind the enemy of the omnipotence of God and the soon coming defeat of all evil spirits. We have provided these Scriptures for you in this book. You can add others to employ in your own personal spiritual warfare.

We should declare authority over the enemy. If you have a good Christian friend, then conduct your spiritual warfare together. Remember, the Bible tells us that one can put a thousand to flight, but two can put ten thousand to flight. There is huge, extra power in our prayer unity.

When Jesus confronted satan face to face, He never tried to reason with him, nor did He waste time yelling. Satan, knowing that Jesus had just fasted for 40 days, said, "If you be the Son of God, command that these stones become bread." But Jesus answered with the Word, "It is written, 'Man shall not live by bread alone, but by every word that proceedeth out of the mouth of God' " (see Mt. 4:3-4). The Word stopped the devil.

At another time the devil took Jesus to the top of the Mount of Temptation above Jericho. He pointed out all the kingdoms and the glory of the world. The devil offered them all to Jesus if only He would but bow down and worship him. But Jesus said, "Away with you, Satan! For it is written, 'You shall worship the Lord your God and Him only shall you serve' " (see Mt. 4:8-10).

The devil then took Jesus up to the pinnacle of the temple in Jerusalem and said, "If You are the Son of God, throw Yourself down. For it is written, 'He shall give His angels charge over You,' and 'In their hands they shall bear You up, lest You dash Your foot against a stone.' " But Jesus again answered with the Word, "It is written again, 'You shall not tempt the Lord your God' " (see Mt. 4:5-7). Satan was utterly defeated by the Word in each instance.

As you prepare to do battle against the enemy, remember that it is important to first *prepare* for war. Singing battle songs that proclaim Christ as a mighty Warrior is very powerful. Worship out loud in the Spirit. Then ask God to search your heart so that you might ask forgiveness for any hidden sin. Finally, ask God for an anointing and infilling of His power.

We hope by now you are convinced that passivity can no longer be tolerated in our Christian walk, or the devil will walk right over us. Therefore, now that we are prepared for battle, shake off the rust and the dust. It's time to strike the enemy with the Guns of God! We are destined for victory!

When you begin to pray intercessory prayers or engage in spiritual warfare, you must learn another secret to ensure your success. There is nothing worse than praying and praying and seeing no results, is there?

Some time back I was called at night to a nearby hospital to pray over a heartbreaking tragedy. A mother had just given birth to her fifth child and she was devastated. Among their first four children, two had been born blind.

Now the fifth, beautiful two-day-old baby lying there was also blind. They just couldn't handle this newest catastrophe and, in desperation, called for prayer. Some 20 minutes after I arrived, I anointed the little blind person with oil. I bound the spirit of blindness and loosed the little baby's sight and then thanked God for his healing and left.

About noon on the following day I received a call. They excitedly announced that the baby could see. I almost jumped through the phone and shouted praises to God! They then said that their doctor had rechecked the baby and told them that he must have made a mistake in saying that the baby was blind.

Oh, how it grieves God when we attribute His mighty works to being the works of man or the devil! These parents doubted God's love and His ability and willingness to answer their prayer, which is near blasphemy. To this day their two other children are still blind.

Always thank God when a prayer is answered. Don't be talked out of it or fear to testify of God's great hand. Then your prayer success will soar!

There will be frequent times when we will experience a quick answer to our prayers. At other times, however, victory won't burst forth in an hour. We are urged by the

Lord to pray and keep on praying. Remember when Daniel dispatched an urgent prayer heavenward. The archangel Michael went forth immediately bringing the answer. But Michael encountered satan's prince of Persia, and the ensuing battle between the two of them delayed the victory 21 days (see Dan. 10:12-13). The important thing to remember, however, is that Daniel continued to pray, and the victory came.

Chapter 8

The Rush Toward Eternity

Suddenly, the rock I stood on started vibrating. The great valley below was filled with the roar and shrieks of two F16 fighters streaking at supersonic speed across the plains of Meggido. I watched enthralled as they climbed straight up and out of sight.

It set my heart pounding and quickened my expectations concerning the dramatic events that will soon take place right there!

I was standing, as I love to do, at the top of Solomon's Stables in Israel where your eyes can take in all the plains of Armageddon and where the Bible tells us the cataclysmic and final war will soon take place. This is the very spot where millions from the far East, from Russia, from North Africa, from Europe and Turkey will send their armies to either fight on the side of God or on the side of satan.

They will battle with every killing tool created by the mind of man. We are told that the carnage becomes so severe that men and horses will wade through blood to their waists. Those powerful Israeli jets, with a star of David on each one, quickened my mind to grasp the imminence of that Armageddon war.

When Jesus was ministering along the shores of Galilee one morning, He came upon a cluster of His followers. They were studying the clouds and were trying to feel which way the wind was blowing. When Jesus reached them, He gently scolded, "Why do you stand here trying to forecast what the weather will be like tomorrow? How much more should you discern the signs of the times?" (see Mt. 16:3).

Let's consider a few things that the Lord has revealed to us that we might not be taken unaware by the sudden closing of this age. The Lord says, "The secret things belong unto the Lord our God: but those things which are revealed belong unto us and to our children for ever" (Deut. 29:29a).

We are told that when the Lord's coming is near, satan will go about as a roaring lion, seeking as many as possible to devour (see 1 Pet. 5:8). This foretells the vast increase in satanic activity now on the earth because the devil knows he has but a short time. Today there is an enormous multiplication of false religions, satan worshipers, mosques, fortune tellers, witch doctors, witches' covens, gurus, and human sacrifices.

An example would be that demonic cult in Japan that openly brags that they worship the god of destruction. They have brewed enormous vats of deadly nerve gas and biological warfare ingredients called Anthrax. This is one of the most deadly poisons known to man. The devil has told them to kill millions and millions of people.

The Bible tells us that in the end-times there will be wars and rumors of wars. Today we have wars in Russia, India, Bosnia, Algeria, Iraq, and a number of African nations. Forty-seven wars are being waged in our world.

There are also more than 100 signs, that the Lord said would occur, whereby we would know that the closing of this age is upon us. Most have already come to pass exactly as God said they would. We are privileged to live in the most exciting moment in all human history!

Now we can move back to my favorite spot overlooking the plains of Meggido. When I look up from there I realize that at almost any time the most thrilling sight man has ever witnessed will take place. Let's let God Himself tell us about the moment we've all been waiting for.

And I saw heaven opened, and behold a white horse; and He that sat upon him was called Faithful and True, and in righteousness He doth judge and make war. His eyes were as a flame of fire, and on His head were many crowns; and He had a name written, that no man knew, but He Himself. And He was clothed with a vesture dipped in blood: and His name is called The Word of God. And the armies which were in heaven followed Him upon white horses, clothed in fine linen, white and clean. And out of His mouth goeth a sharp sword, that with it He should smite the nations: and He shall rule them with a rod of iron: and He treadeth the winepress of the fierceness and wrath of Almighty God. And He hath on His vesture and on His thigh a name written, KING OF KINGS, AND LORD OF LORDS. ... And I saw the beast, and the kings of the earth, and their armies, gathered together to make war against Him that sat on the horse, and against His army. And the beast was taken, and with him the false prophet that wrought miracles before him, with which he deceived them that had received the mark of the beast, and them that worshipped his image.

These both were cast alive into a lake of fire burning with brimstone. And the remnant were slain with the sword of Him that sat upon the horse, which sword proceeded out of His mouth: and all the fowls were filled with their flesh. And I saw an angel come down from heaven, having the key of the bottomless pit and a great chain in his hand. And he laid hold on the dragon, that old serpent, which is the Devil, and Satan, and bound him a thousand years, and cast him into the bottomless pit, and shut him up, and set a seal upon him, that he should deceive the nations no more, till the thousand years should be fulfilled: and after that he must be loosed a little season (Revelation 19:11-16,19–20:3).

And so, what will Jesus do next? He continues over the next few seconds to streak toward the Mount of Olives overlooking Jerusalem. He walks down through the Valley of Kiddron and passes straight through the Golden Gate. This gate has been carefully sealed up with stones and cement by the Muslims. This will not deter our King of kings for a moment. He will look at it and it will swing open to allow Him to walk across the Temple Mount and up to Mount Zion. There He will sit upon His throne and commence His rule over the whole earth with us for 1,000 glorious years.

Everything we detest will be cast from our planet like so many filthy rags. He will throw them off the earth forever, and what He throws into the trash bin of the universe you will never want again.

He banishes all war, cancer, pain, all sickness, loneliness, crime, hatred, death, ugliness, and poverty. There will be no more blindness. No one will be crippled from that moment on. No more heartache. No more bills. No more door locks. The lamb will lie down with the lion, and all the forest animals will be reconciled with us. You see, when Jesus comes through that door above the battle of Armageddon, He will freeze-frame all further death, hatred, and war. Good riddance!

Once our King is in residence all will be more than well. But between now and then it is our responsibility to begin to wage spiritual warfare against all the demonic forces and fallen angels who pollute this earth and delay His arrival. We shall come against them with the Word of God that weakens and binds them terribly. It is our assignment through spiritual warfare to prepare the way of the Lord. He backs us *today*! He binds in Heaven whatever we bind here on earth and He looses in Heaven whatsoever we loose in our spiritual warfare.

Finally, my brethren, be strong in the Lord, and in the power of His might. Put on the whole armour of God, that ye may be able to stand against the wiles of the devil. For we wrestle not against flesh and blood, but against principalities, against powers, against the rulers of the darkness of this world, against spiritual [hosts of] *wickedness in* [heavenly] *places. Wherefore take unto you the whole armour of God, that ye may be able to withstand in the evil day, and having done all, to stand. Stand therefore, having* [girded your waist] *with truth, and having on the breastplate of righteousness; and your feet shod with the preparation of the gospel of peace; above all, taking the shield of faith, wherewith ye shall be able to quench all the fiery darts of the wicked* [one]. *And take the helmet of salvation, and the sword of the Spirit, which is the word of God* (Ephesians 6:10-17).

Let's buckle on our armor, pick up our spiritual weapons, and make war over the enemy!

It is the time to take the Kingdom
Rise up ye strong, 'tis Christ's command
For every power and every Kingdom
Is given now into your hand.

He that hath ears to hear the Trumpet
He that hath heart to understand
It is the time to take the Kingdom
Rise up ye strong, possess the land.

Chapter 9

The Golden Sunrise!

Now the twentieth century rages forward. It marks the deadliest, stormiest, and most despairing years ever. But look—there's a cloud forming on the horizon—but this time it's a golden one! Good times are headed for this planet, and all the king's horses and all the devil's angels can't stop it!

"...Behold, one like the Son of man came with the clouds of heaven.... And there was given Him dominion, and glory, and a kingdom, that all people, nations, and languages, should serve Him: His dominion is an everlasting dominion, which shall not pass away, and His kingdom that which shall not be destroyed" (Dan. 7:13-14). Our King is about to appear as vindicator of His Word and vindicator of His people, which is all the more reason why we must stand and fight wielding the Guns of God as we see the ushering in of God's Kingdom. The time is so short, and the harvest is still so great!

For endless centuries men have dreamed of creating an ideal world, a Shangri-La. First the Babylonians, then the Egyptians, the Greeks and the Romans; all followed, in more recent times, by the British, the Nazis, the Communists, and even the Americans. Each had a frenetic drive to usher in their own brand of utopia. But one after another has ended in dust, smoke, slavery, or despair.

There are still some jarring ruts ahead as humanity road stretches toward that golden Millennium horizon. Now, more than ever, the army of God must be trained and equipped to fight the enemy of men's souls. Today the world is convulsing from a terminal case of "sin-fever." Things are getting pretty "hairy"—inflation, drugs, moral corruption, and terrorists shopping for atomic bombs. Something big is in the air, and even a fool can sense the game is about up.

Masses are groping for either salvation or suicide. Some try to drown their despair with drugs and alcohol. Why?

In decades past, orators could weave a compelling tapestry of a glowing future for mankind: "Through education and skyrocketing technology, a chicken in every pot, two cars in every garage, unheard of prosperity—see it just ahead!"

But that future finally arrived, and instead of being the glittering one, it was leaden: Hiroshima, Berlin, Bosnia, the Holocaust, and the Golan Heights. The twentieth century staggers set in—the fate of our planet hangs in the balance. The orators' golden horizons have turned ominously gray.

A perplexed world stands leaderless and faint. The Bible warns against just such uncertainty: "[Without a] vision, the people perish" (Prov. 29:18a).

And so, in the dusk of a dying age, that newly-forming golden cloud is a sight to behold! Man's phony virtual reality is about to become Christ's stark reality. The good news of Millennium reality must now be heralded—its wonders polished to an accurate brilliance. The Kingdom Age, with Jesus at its helm, is the very super-world that has eluded civilization while man has been at the steering wheel of life.

We must bring its nearness into focus. Just look at it: vibrancy, rest, peace, dancing, and laughter—peace on earth, good will toward men.

I can already see Millennium through that colossal door called "time," which is now, irreversibly, swinging open. Jesus is the Door, and He's calling to the people on our smoking planet, "I offer life—abundant and eternal! Hurry. Don't waste time looking for another way into super-world Kingdom. I am the only Way. Come, the Millennium bells are ringing...."

Believers must sound the very good news that the way is still open for the lost. We must compel them to safety before the way closes. It's the hour to let the Holy Spirit ignite one last spiritual revolution. The fire of the early Church must be rekindled! But how do we do that? By employing the Guns of God in fervent intercession to God for the souls of men, and by binding the enemy's hold on sinful humanity as we intercede to God for them.

Those Book-of-Acts Christians weren't ashamed to be identified with their leader, Jesus Christ. Eleven of the 12 Apostles willingly died for our cause. Their Spirit-inspired zeal turned the world upside down. Jesus is worth making spiritual revolution for! "Behold, the Lord cometh with ten thousands of His saints" (Jude 14b).

It's time to change—we're on a sinking world. Why hide the Jesus-Lifeboat? We need to "go public" with the news of Jesus' Kingdom, but to do that we must become fearless warriors, engaging and defeating the enemy at every point of confrontation.

The lost seem to have lost all fear of God, but it's no time to "stonewall" against God. Soon the swingers and the do-your-own-thingers will discover—one heartbeat too late—that Jesus isn't the emaciated, effeminate, pitiful, dead figure on the crucifix. Their laughter will freeze as they face a blazing-eyed, omnipotent, brilliant, authoritative, live Jesus. "...And I will not [allow] them [to] pollute My holy name any more..." (Ezek. 39:7).

It's time to go radical for righteousness, to declare war against sin and satan, to "make waves" for Jesus! Never again shall we be timid about our allegiance to that One who hung the stars in space! We're His authorized representatives—His agents on this planet. Let our blood run hot against sin!

"I will not rest, until the righteousness thereof go forth as brightness, and the salvation thereof as a lamp that burneth" (Is. 62:1b). Yes, "mine eyes have seen the glory of the coming of the Lord...."

It is time to sound the final alert for all desiring Millennium passports. Planet earth is about to be born again! "The kingdoms of this world [will very soon] become the kingdoms of our Lord, and of His Christ; and He shall reign for ever and ever" (Rev. 11:15b).

Those early streaks in the eastern sky herald Millennium dawn—a romantic 1,000-year-long valentine from a loving God. Will we be satisfied to keep that valentine to ourselves and to stand by and allow the devil to pull thousands down into the smoking abyss with him, or will we put on the full armor of God and fight, snatching the lost from the very gates of hell?

Shall we be mere spectators of the great wheels and gears cranking this corrupt world toward time's end? No, no, we must be participants and proud activists in closing this satan-corrupted age! You see, enlistment in God's army isn't an option. You were drafted the moment you were saved! The question is, will you fight? Will you lock arms with your fellow soldiers of the cross and proclaim the mighty Word of God, keeping the Guns of God blazing every step of the way? I challenge you to do that. And I declare to you with all the passion in my heart, as a born-again, blood-washed, Spirit-filled believer, you have no other choice!

"For Thine is the kingdom, and the power, and the glory, for ever. Amen" (Mt. 6:13b).

Don't Quit

When things go wrong, as they sometimes will,
When the road you're trudging seems all up hill,
When the funds are low, and the debts are high,
And you want to smile but you have to sigh,
When care is pressing you down a bit,
Rest if you must, but don't quit.

Life is queer with its twists and turns,
As everyone of us sometimes learns,
And many a failure turns about,
When he might have won had he stuck it out,
Don't give up though the pace seems slow,
You may succeed with another blow.

Success is failure turned inside out,
The silver tint of the clouds of doubt,
And you never can tell how close you are,
It may be near when it seems so far,
So stick to the fight when you're hardest hit,
It's when things seems worse
That you must not quit.

Author Unknown

Saga of the Chief Musician

Earlier this year, Christine Darg and I were on a ten-day ministry campaign in Britain. Our music leader was Brenda Taylor. Both the congregation and our ministry team grew with excitement over the messages God gave on spiritual warfare. Brenda was also deeply touched. One night, after the meeting, she remained in the room playing her beautiful electronic piano. God also seemed to be touched by the words brought forth and gave Brenda this song, "The Guns of God." This song became the theme of the entire campaign.

Index of
Scriptural Ammunition

Wage strong warfare, as Paul admonished Timothy, with the following Scriptures. If your dilemma is not mentioned here, ask the Holy Spirit to give you a verse, and He will be faithful to teach you. He is your precious Helper!

Let these verses become *rhema* (enlightened words) as you send them forth out of your mouth. See the Word as an active force that, once sent forth, will return like a boomerang, never void, but having accomplished and brought the answer! As declared in Isaiah 55:11, it will complete that purpose for which it is sent, and it shall prosper!

ABILITY: Philippians 4:13; 1 Corinthians 1:30; 2:16; 12:7; Exodus 31:3-4; Romans 12:6

Decree: Defeat is nailed to the cross. I can do all things through Christ. The Holy Spirit's personality and gift potentialities are within me. Like Bezaleel (see Ex. 31:1-4) of old, I have the Holy Spirit who imparts to me wisdom, understanding, and knowledge in workmanship. The Holy Spirit is more than enough to put me over in any situation or circumstance. He gives me "inside information."

ABORTION (if considering): Deuteronomy 30:19; Matthew 18:10-14

Command and Decree: Spirit of death and destruction and spirit of the age of the love of many waxing cold, I command you and your lies to leave me. I dare to choose life in Jesus' name. Together, Lord, we shall birth this child, whom I dedicate in the womb to Your glory. May the birth and life of this child bring great shame to the enemy who plotted to take its life!

ABORTION (past): Matthew 12:31; Psalm 103:2-3; 1 John 1:9

Confession: Lord, with great sorrow of heart I have repented for the sin of murder, and now I confess that there is no condemnation to those who are in Christ Jesus.

Command: Spirit of murder and rebellion, leave us now in Jesus' name!

ACCIDENTS: Psalm 91:1-3,11-12; Job 1:10; Genesis 15:1b

Decree: The Lord shields me continually from accidents. He has put a protective hedge about me and my house and everything that I own.

ADVANCED AGE: Psalm 92:14; 103:5

Decree: I decree that even in my old age, my youth is renewed like the eagle's and my life shall still bring forth fruit.

ALCOHOLISM/ADDICTIONS: Psalm 103:3; 107:20; Jeremiah 31:11

Command: Addiction, leave me! Demons of alcohol and addiction, do not dominate me. I dominate and resist them in Jesus' mighty and victorious name!

ANGELIC MINISTRY: Psalm 34:7; Hebrews 1:14; Matthew 18:10

Decree: The angelic hosts are my companions and defenders!

ARMOR OF GOD: Isaiah 59:17; Ephesians 6:14-17

Decree: I have put on the armor of God to use as both defensive and offensive weaponry. It has been put on to stay as long as I live in this world!

ARTHRITIS: Isaiah 66:14

Decree: I forgive all my enemies. I am a child of God. I do not allow any root of bitterness in my life. Arthritis was nailed to the cross, and it has no legal place in my body.

ASTHMA: Isaiah 42:5; Acts 17:25b

Command: Spirit of infirmity, leave me in Jesus' name. I bind you and cut off all generational ties that have passed through my family line in Jesus' name.

AUTHORITY (spiritual): Matthew 16:19; 28:19; Luke 10:19; Mark 16:17

Decree: All authority in heaven and in earth has been given to my Lord Jesus, and He shares His authority with me. Nothing shall by any means hurt me. Satan is the god of this world, but he is not my master. He must obey the believer's voice, in Jesus' name.

BACK TROUBLE: Isaiah 53:4

Decree: He gave His back to the smiters, and by His stripes I was healed.

BARRENNESS: Deuteronomy 7:14; Psalm 113:9; Luke 1:38,45

Decree: Barrenness is a curse. Jesus became a curse for me so that I might have life. Let it be done unto me and my husband according to the Word of God. I am blessed because I believe that there shall be a performance of the promise of God's Word.

BEAUTY: Isaiah 61:1-3; Psalm 90:17; Judges 5:31

Decree: Charm is deceitful and worldly beauty is vain (see Proverbs 31:30), but I am clothed in the beauty of the Lord. I shine as the sun in full strength because the Sun of righteousness has arisen upon me with healing in His wings (see Malachi 4:2) and I reflect His glory!

BLEEDING (hemorrhaging): Mark 5:29; Matthew 9:22; Acts 28:8

Declaration: My faith has made me whole. (Also see proclamation concerning blood disorders.)

BLINDNESS: Psalm 146:8; Isaiah 35:5; Matthew 11:4-5

Decree: Blindness is listed as part of the curse of the law in Deuteronomy 28:28; therefore, it has no legal place on a child of the New Covenant.

Command: Spirit of blindness, leave now in Jesus' name. I command the eyes to open at the Word of the Lord!

BLOOD DISORDERS (blood pressure, diseases, diabetes, anemia, hypoglycemia, etc.): Mark 5:29; Ezekiel 16:6; Romans 3:25a

Proclamation: The blood of Jesus has made an atonement for our souls, and that blessed atonement includes healing, for it is by His wounds that we have been healed.

We are justified by His blood (see Romans 5:9); we have redemption through and by His blood (see Ephesians 1:7; 1 Peter 1:19). He took His own blood into the Holy of Holies and it has not lost its power. By the wounds of Jesus I am healed. The eternal wounds in His side and in His hands and feet are substitutes for my wounds, infirmities, and sicknesses. Because the Savior bears wounds, I do not have to. Hallelujah! What a Savior!

BOLDNESS: Proverbs 28:1; Hebrews 4:16; Ephesians 6:19-20

Proclamation: I am bold as a lion. I am waxing more bold in Jesus' name. Because I am the righteousness of God in Christ Jesus, I am bold toward God, bold toward man—refusing the fear of man—and bold toward devils.

BROKEN HEART: Psalm 34:18; Isaiah 61:1

Decree: There is a balm in the name of Jesus. His name is ointment poured out to heal in this situation.

BRUISES/SCARS: Isaiah 43:2; Job 33:25

Decree: Let it (healing) be unto me according to Your Word!

CANCER: Deuteronomy 28:27; Galatians 3:13; Psalm 103:2-3; James 5:14-15; Proverbs 4:20-22; Isaiah 53:5; 1 Peter 2:24; Mark 11:21-23; 16:18; Matthew 8:2-3

Proclamation: I speak out loud and address the spirit of cancer: you are cursed in Jesus' name. I speak to this mountain (problem) and command it to be removed. A thousand may fall by my side, but it will not come near me. Thank You, Lord, that You said to the leper, "I WILL." Thank You, Lord, that You are willing to heal me.

CHILDREN: 1 Samuel 3:9; Acts 2:17; Isaiah 49:25; 54:13; Proverbs 22:6; Lamentations 2:19; Psalm 112:1-2; Daniel 1:4,17; Ephesians 6:1-4; Numbers 6:24-26

Decree: I surround my children with faith rather than fear. They shall be mighty upon the earth. They shall be the head and not the tail. They shall not depart from the ways of the Lord. A blessing is commanded upon the children of the upright. My children obey their parents; therefore, things will go well with them. My sons and daughters shall prophesy and they shall see visions. They are skillful in all wisdom and have understanding in science and knowledge in all learning. Great is their peace! Lord, I put Your name upon my children.

COURT CASES: Luke 12:12; 21:14-15

Decree: I decree the justice of God Almighty shall prevail in this case. No weapon formed against me shall prosper, for this is the heritage of the servants of the Lord (see Isaiah 54:17).

CURSES: Genesis 12:3; Proverbs 26:2; Galatians 3:13-14

Decree: I break every curse in the name of Jesus against my life and the lives of my family and children. I fear no curse of man, because the causeless curse cannot alight on me or my household.

DEAFNESS (spirit of): Matthew 11:5; Mark 9:25; 16:17

Command: I rebuke you, foul spirit of deafness, and cast you out in Jesus' name.

DEATH (spirit of): Psalm 33:18-19; 118:17

Command: Spirit of death, I bind you in Jesus' name and cast you out!

DEMONS: Mark 16:17; Luke 10:19; Revelation 12:11; Psalm 110:2; Ephesians 4:27; James 4:7; 1 Peter 5:8-9

Declaration: I will resist the devil as often as is necessary, and he will continually be on the run. I cast out demons in Jesus' name. They do not rule me. I rule in the midst of my enemies to pluck up and to plant. I have been translated out of the kingdom of darkness into His glorious light.

DEPRESSION: Psalm 42:11; 57:7; Isaiah 61:3

Decree: I train myself to command my soul to return to a normal state as the psalmist did. Command: Spirit of depression and destruction, I resist you and bind you in Jesus' name. I cast you out!

DIVINE HEALTH: Exodus 15:26; 23:25; Proverbs 4:20,22; Job 42:10,12; Matthew 6:10; 8:16-17; Hebrews 10:7; 2 Chronicles 16:12b; Jeremiah 17:5; 1 Kings 8:56

Decree: Precious Jesus, You did not carry my infirmities and sicknesses in vain. I purpose to appropriate the divine health that You paid the awful price to purchase. You, Lord, are my Great Physician. I will not make the mistake of King Asa, who consulted physicians without consulting You. I take You as my Healer and thank You that healing is part of the Atonement. I purpose to walk in divine health. I train myself to resist every assault of sickness in Jesus' name. As soon as symptoms are detected, I will not tolerate them. I will not take the path of least resistance, but I will steadfastly resist satan in Jesus' name. I will contend for my health. I will not let Your words drop to the ground. Thank You, Jesus, that You came to do the will of the Father and that it is His will that we be well.

DRUG ADDICTION: John 8:36; Psalm 107:20; Isaiah 61:1; Luke 4:18

Command: Spirit of addiction, I bind and cast you out in Jesus' name!

EMOTIONAL DISORDERS: 2 Timothy 1:7; 1 Corinthians 2:16

Declaration: We have the mind of Christ.

EVANGELISM (command and promises): Matthew 28:18-20; Mark 1:17, 16:15-18; Acts 1:8; Proverbs 11:30b; Psalm 2:8; Luke 5:4b; 10:2; Joel 3:14; Isaiah 41:14-15; John 14:12

Decree: Since evangelism is God's number one priority, I shall obey the Great Commission. Father, I ask You for entire nations in Jesus' name. I shall do the greater works that You promised because You ascended to the Father and sent the Holy Spirit as my Helper and Co-Laborer.

FAITH: Mark 9:23; Romans 4:20; 10:17; 14:23b; Hebrews 11:1,6; 6:12; Matthew 9:22; 1 Peter 1:7; James 1:3

Decree: I will live by my faith. I will also teach my children that faith pleases God. I will not be moved by my senses but only by the Word of God. The trial of my faith is more precious than gold. The trial of my faith is also working patience in me. I refuse to panic because I am adding patience to my faith. Like Abraham, I stagger not at the promise of God through unbelief, but I am strong in faith, giving glory to God. With my "faith gun" I shall overcome this world system!

FALLS (physical and spiritual): Proverbs 16:18; Jude 24; Job 4:4; Psalm 37:23-24; 56:13

Decree: Though I may fall, because God upholds me with His hand, I will not be utterly cast down, but I will arise and walk in the ordered steps of a righteous man.

FARMING: Deuteronomy 28:3; Psalm 85:12

Decree: I am blessed in the field, and my land shall yield increase.

FASTING: Matthew 6:16-18; 17:21

Decree: I will fast and pray obediently and in secret before the Lord, and He shall reward me openly.

FAVOR: Psalm 5:12; 84:11; Proverbs 11:27; John 12:26; Esther 2:15,17; Luke 2:52

Decree: I am growing in favor both with God and man. I shall obtain favor in the sight of all who look upon me.

FEAR: 2 Timothy 1:7; Psalm 23:4; 91:5; 118:6; Joshua 1:9; Proverbs 29:25; Job 3:25; 2 Chronicles 20:15

Decree: I reject the spirit of fear. I do not greatly fear any disease or any problem because the name of Jesus is greater than any disease or any problem. I am strong in the Lord and I am not afraid. Jesus has set me free from the fear of any devil or any man.

FEVER: Luke 4:38-39

Rebuke: Fever, I rebuke you in Jesus' name!

GUIDANCE: John 16:13; Romans 8:14; Psalm 32:8-9; Proverbs 4:18

Decree: The Lord guides me into all truth. I am led by the Spirit of God. I am sensitive to the slightest movement of His eye. Therefore I am not like a stubborn mule that must be prodded by bit and bridle. I do not stumble through life without purpose; rather, my path is increasingly enlightened.

HOLINESS: Proverbs 22:11; Hebrews 12:14

Decree: I am clothed in the holiness of God Himself!

HOMOSEXUALITY: Leviticus 20:13; John 8:11b

Command: Spirit of perversity, I bind you and cast you out in Jesus' name, and I forbid you never to return to torment. Go to the uninhabited places until Judgment Day!

HUMILITY: Proverbs 22:4; 1 Peter 5:6; James 4:6
Decree: I declare that I shall humble myself in God's sight, and He will lift me up.

IDLENESS: Proverbs 31:27
Decree: I do not eat the bread of idleness!

IMMUNITY (strong immune system): Psalm 27:1; 91:7; Exodus 23:25
Decree: I do not need to fear sickness or infirmity for God is the strength of my life and He has taken sickness from my midst.

INFECTIONS: Isaiah 53:4a
Decree: Spirit of infirmity, you have no place in my life because I am a child of God, redeemed from the curse. Therefore I command you to leave in Jesus' name!

INSOMNIA: Psalm 3:5; 4:8; Proverbs 3:24
Decree: My sleep is sweet according to the Word of the Lord.

INTERCESSORS: Jeremiah 9:17-18; Lamentations 2:19; Joel 2:17; Romans 8:26-27
Decree: I decree that I shall rise from my bed and cry out in the night, that the Lord will hear me and answer me, even before I speak.

JOY: Philippians 4:4; Proverbs 17:22; Nehemiah 8:10c; Romans 14:17; John 16:22c
Declaration: I will daily stir up the fruit of the Spirit called "joy." I permit no man to rob me of my joy. I give thanks in everything. As I go out to the battle singing praises to my God, He promises to ambush the enemy for me.

LEUKEMIA: Proverbs 3:7-8

Decree: Because I am not wise in my own eyes and because I fear the Lord, I have departed from evil, and God has renewed my health and the marrow in my bones.

LIES/LYING SPIRIT: Psalm 119:104

Decree: I purpose in my heart to order my conversation aright. I purpose to let the meditation of my heart and the words of my mouth be acceptable in the sight of God!

LONELINESS: Psalm 68:6a; Matthew 28:20b; Hebrews 13:5b

Decree: Because God has declared that He will never leave or forsake me, I know that I am never alone.

MARITAL HARMONY: Jeremiah 32:39; Amos 3:3; Ecclesiastes 4:9-12; Proverbs 18:22; 19:14b; 31:10-12,23

Decree: God has given us one heart and one way, to walk together and to be a blessing to our children after us forever.

MATERIAL NEEDS: Genesis 22:8-14; Philippians 4:19

Confession: I never lack anything because Jehovah Jireh is my Source. Because I give, it is also given unto me (see Luke 6:38).

OCCULT (abominations to God): Deuteronomy 18:10-11; Jeremiah 44:8; Isaiah 47:12-13

Declaration: I renounce all these works of darkness and satan. Even the elect of God will be deceived, if it were possible; therefore, I purpose in my heart to expose these works of darkness with the Word of God.

PAIN: Isaiah 53:4b

Decree: Because Jesus has borne my sorrows (pains), I am free from pain and sorrow.

PEACE: 1 Peter 5:7; Isaiah 53:5

Decree: I can walk in peace because I have cast all my cares on the One who cares for me. Jesus bore the chastisement needful to obtain my peace.

PRAISE: Psalm 34:1; 113:3; 119:164

Declaration: I will praise the Lord more and more. Instead of fretting, I will praise Him. My high praises will bind spiritual rulers in fetters of iron.

PRAYER (power of): Philippians 4:6b; James 5:16b; 1 John 5:14-15; 1 Thessalonians 5:17; Jude 20

Proclamation: The Word says I am the righteousness of God in Christ Jesus. Therefore I am legally righteous and my fervent prayers avail much!

PROMOTION: Proverbs 18:12b,16; Psalm 23:5; 37:34-37; 75:6-7

Decree: You prepare a table before me in the presence of my enemies, therefore I have favor and walk in Your promotion.

PROSPERITY: 3 John 2; Psalm 23:5c-6; 122:6; Malachi 3:10-11a; Proverbs 3:9-10

Decree: The blessing of the Lord is upon me, my cup runs over. Because I honor the Lord with my substance and with the firstfruits of all my increase, I am filled with plenty!

REAPING (law of sowing and reaping): 2 Corinthians 9:6; Galatians 6:9

Decree: I will not grow weary in doing well. Because I sow bountifully, I shall also reap bountifully!

SENILITY: 2 Timothy 1:7; Psalm 105:37b; Hebrews 13:8

Decree: Because I have a sound mind, I will not fear senility, for there was not one feeble person among all the tribes of Israel, and Jesus Christ is the same yesterday, today and forever.

SKIN CANCER/SKIN DISORDERS: Psalm 42:11; 121:5-6; Proverbs 4:22
Decree: God's Word is medicine to all my flesh.

SMOKING: John 5:14; James 4:7
Decree: The Holy Spirit who lives within me now gives me a holy distaste for all types of tobacco. I will not pollute the atmosphere of this temple of God, nor will I be so inconsiderate as to violate the air space of others. No matter how many times the devil tries to reoccupy this refurbished temple, I will resist him in Jesus' name. I thank You, Lord, that new tissue will grow to replace my blackened lungs. Thank You for having mercy upon me and protecting me from all lung cancer. According to my faith it shall be unto me.

STRENGTH: Deuteronomy 33:25b; Ephesians 6:10; Joshua 1:7,9; Daniel 11:32b; Psalm 84:5-7
Decree: I am moving from strength to strength.

SUCCESS: Joshua 1:5,8; Psalm 1:1-3; Judges 5:31; Daniel 11:32b
Decree: Meditation in Your Word builds success into my spirit. I shall do exploits for Jesus today. Because I love the Lord, I shall shine as the sun in full strength.

TEETH: Song of Solomon 4:2
Decree: My teeth are white and even and healthy.

TONGUE: Proverbs 6:2; 12:18; 13:3; 18:21; Mark 11:23
Decree: I set a guard over my mouth and order my conversation aright.

TRAVEL: Psalm 121:8; Exodus 33:14
Decree: The Lord's presence is with me wherever I go.

TROUBLE: Jeremiah 33:3; Psalm 34:17,19; 46:1; 50:15; 66:12; 119:71; 1 Peter 1:7

Decree: The trial of my faith is more precious than gold. My faith is strengthened through trials. I am not immune from trials in this sinstained world; however, my God promises to deliver me out of all of them!

WEAKNESS: Deuteronomy 34:7; Psalm 105:37; Zechariah 12:8b; Isaiah 35:3-4; Joshua 14:11

Decree: Because God is on my side, I say that I am strong! I refuse to become feeble. I will not equate growing old with feebleness. I will not plan nor make provisions to be feeble. I shall be as David and his mighty men. I also purpose to be like Joshua and Caleb who at the age of 85 inherited the Promised Land.

WEARINESS: Isaiah 40:29

Decree: God gives me power and He increases my strength.

WISDOM: James 1:5

Decree: I ask the Lord daily for wisdom, and He gives wisdom to me liberally. He is increasing wisdom.

Powerful Weapons for Victory

God's Word; the whole armor of God; the authority to invoke the name and the blood of Jesus; the power of the Holy Spirit; the gift of faith; protection and intervention by God's messenger angels; the gifts of the Spirit—these are our weapons for victory!

REMEMBER:

For the weapons of our warfare are not carnal, but mighty through God to the pulling down of strong holds (2 Corinthians 10:4).

Powerful Bullets for Your Guns of God

"Surely the Lord God will do nothing, but He revealeth His secret unto His servants the prophets" (Amos 3:7).

"For the Word of God is quick, and powerful, and sharper than any twoedged sword..." (Heb. 4:12).

With His Word God spoke the world and the heavens into being (see Gen. 1).

Jesus always answered satan, "It is written!" (see Mt. 4).

"With God, all things are possible" (see Mt. 19:26).

Whatsoever thou shalt bind on earth shall be bound in heaven: and whatsoever thou shalt loose on earth shall be loosed in heaven" (Mt. 16:19b).

Every healing prayer and every rebuke to dark forces triumphed as Jesus ministered (see the Gospels).

During His Galilee ministry He healed them all and He healed them utterly (see the Gospels).

Then Jesus said, "And greater things shall you do" (see Jn. 14:12).

"Behold, I give unto you power...over all the power of the enemy..." (Lk. 10:19).

Jesus came to defeat satan (see 1 Jn. 3:8).

Satan is the prince of liars (see Jn. 8:44).

Satan comes "to steal, and to kill, and to destroy" (Jn. 10:10).

"And the gates of hell *shall not* prevail against [us]" (Mt. 16:18b).

Jesus said, "Go and cast out demons" (see Mt. 10:8).

God says we are to "stand in the gap [for My people]" (see Ezek. 22:30).

"Our Father which art in heaven...Thy will be done in earth, as it is in heaven" (see Mt. 6:9-13).

God cast lucifer, the demons, and all evil angels out of heaven (see Rev. 12:4).

They will be bound and cast into a bottomless pit when Christ returns (see Rev. 20:2-3).

Jesus said, "...Whatsoever ye shall ask in My name, that will I do" (Jn. 14:13a).

Jesus intercedes for and with us from heaven (see Heb. 7:25).

Jesus is the Captain of the Lord of Hosts (see Josh. 5:14-15).

We do not fight "against flesh and blood [people], but against principalities, against powers, against the rulers of the darkness of this world, against spiritual wickedness in [the air—evil spirits]" (Eph. 6:12b).

"Put on the whole armour of God, that ye may be able to stand against the [evils] of the devil" (Eph. 6:11).

"And from the days of John the Baptist until now the kingdom of heaven suffereth violence, *and the violent take it by force*" (Mt. 11:12).

"For God hath not given us the spirit of fear; but of [peace] power... and of a sound mind" (2 Tim. 1:7).

"Submit yourselves therefore to God. Resist the devil, and he will flee from you" (Jas. 4:7).

"Again I say unto you, That if two of you shall agree on earth as touching any thing that they shall ask, it shall be done for them of My Father which is in heaven" (Mt. 18:19).

"For the weapons of our warfare are not carnal, but mighty through God to the pulling down of strong holds" (2 Cor. 10:4).

Before the name of Jesus, every knee shall bow (see Phil. 2:10).

One thousand demons were cast out of just one man by Jesus at Gadera; then he became a disciple (see Lk. 8:26-39).

"...[The devil] was a murderer from the beginning, and abode not in the truth, because there is no truth in him. When he speaketh a lie, he speaketh of his own: for he is a liar, and the father of it" (Jn. 8:44).

The devil's future: "And I saw an angel come down from heaven, having the key of the bottomless pit and a great chain in his hand. And he laid hold on the dragon, that old serpent, which is the Devil, and Satan, and bound him a thousand years" (Rev. 20:1-2).

"And they overcame him [satan] by the blood of the Lamb, and by the word of their testimony" (Rev. 12:11a).

"[They who] know their God shall be strong, and do exploits" (Dan. 11:32b).

"...In all these things we are more than conquerors through Him that loved us" (Rom. 8:37).

Jonathan said, "[It] is no restraint to the Lord to save by many or by few" (1 Sam. 14:6b).

"Man doth not live by bread only, but by every word that proceedeth out of the mouth of the Lord..." (Deut. 8:3b).

Early apostles "turned the world upside down" (see Acts 17:6).

"For the Word of God is quick, and powerful, and sharper than any twoedged sword..." (Heb. 4:12).

"He that sitteth in the heavens [laughs]" (Ps. 2:4a).

"For this purpose [Jesus] the Son of God was manifested, that He might destroy the works of the devil" (1 Jn. 3:8b).

"...Having [disarmed] principalities and powers, He made a [public spectacle] of them...triumphing over them in it" (Col. 2:15).

"And the devil that deceived them was cast into the lake of fire and brimstone, where...[he] shall be tormented day and night for ever and ever" (Rev. 20:10).

"Let God arise, let His enemies be scattered" (Ps. 68:1a).

The story of Shadrach, Meshach and Abednego—they could not be burned, and Jesus was seen in the furnace with them (see Dan. 3).

At Caesarea Philipi Jesus declared through Peter, "I give you the keys of the Kingdom" (see Mt. 16:19).

"You armed me with strength for battle" (Ps. 18:39a NIV).

By my God I can leap over a wall (see Ps. 18:29).

"Blessed be the Lord my strength, which teacheth my hands to war, and my fingers to fight" (Ps. 144:1).

God's people are "terrible as an army with banners" (see Song 6:4)!

"Then He called His twelve disciples together, and gave them power and authority over all devils, and to cure diseases" (Lk. 9:1).

"Hast thou not known? hast thou not heard, that the everlasting God, the Lord, the Creator of the ends of the earth, fainteth not, neither is weary? there is no searching of His understanding. He giveth power to the faint; and to them that have no might He increaseth strength. ... But they that wait upon the Lord shall renew their strength; they shall mount up with wings as eagles; they shall run, and not be weary; and they shall walk, and not faint" (Is. 40:28-29,31).

"And whatsoever ye shall ask in My name, that will I do" (Jn. 14:13a).

Professor Johannes Myung Bhum Lee says, "The devil's ultimate weapon for deceiving us into fear and slavery to him is to use the power of death. He threatens us with death but this is also a deception because Jesus already destroyed this power when He arose from death, thereby conquering it. Death has no power over us who are in Christ anymore, but the devil continues to try to deceive us into thinking that he still holds a viable weapon against us."

The Stars Are Falling

A Profound Issue

There is a piece of land only about three miles square that might easily be identifiable as one of the gates of hell here on earth.

They call this dark field "Hollywood." If you were to sit down and invent a concentration of activities to pollute and destroy the morals and the spiritual lives on this earth, you would do it as satan has done. Slowly and subtly, this cancer of evil has evolved under the direction of the devil himself.

Hollywood is not only the capital of the morally corrupt movie industry, but it is also an inciter of violence, rap music, corrupting television, child molestation, prostitution, abortion, pornography, X-rated videos, drug abuse, and rampant homosexuality. Together with the ACLU, the industry has likewise fought against the role of God Himself in our society.

This terrible engine of moral destruction, hiding behind the First Amendment, must be dealt with. Hollywood has such power to communicate, and it is polluting souls of young people throughout the world.

I utterly agree with Senator Bob Dole, Bill Bennett, Pat Robertson, and tens of thousands of pastors in their concerns for the very life of America because of the evil implications from Hollywood.

This is what I want us to do. Today I plead with you to join us in a massive campaign of spiritual warfare and prayer until Hollywood is brought to its knees before God! God is with us!

Through God's awesome foresight, He directed us to build our big California station, KVOH, on Chatsworth Peak. This station is only some 25 miles from Hollywood itself. We can point the antenna direction to fill the air over Hollywood with the Word of God. We want to do spiritual warfare and to minister directly into this evil area hour after hour for as long as it takes.

We must swiftly bind these demonic forces, as well as minister to the people who live in this Sodom and Gomorrah region. The nations of earth will call us blessed when we do. We are all being choked by the deadly sewage flowing out of Hollywood, and we need deliverance!

Join God's Spiritual Task Force

God's spiritual task force is what we are as we apply the substance of this book to our lives. And that includes you! Remember that Christ will go before us and protect us. Jesus is the Captain and the Lord of hosts. When He sees us in a counterattack by the enemy, He can dispatch powerful angels to the rescue.

We also want our Spiritual Strike Force friends to receive, at no charge, our monthly News Reports, that will keep you informed on God's victories around the world.

Recommended Reading

I want to highly recommend that you read the following books to further enhance the Spirit's message in the *Guns of God*:

Warfare Prayer by Dr. C. Peter Wagner
The Last of the Giants by George Otis, Jr.
Possessing the Gates of the Enemy by Cindy Jacobs
The Power and Blessing by Dr. Jack Hayford
The Second Coming by Pat Robertson

About the Author

Dr. George Otis is president and founder of High Adventure Ministries, which operates the Voice of Hope World Radio Network.

George is a descendant of Harrison Gray Otis, the founding publisher of the *Los Angeles Times*, and James Otis, "a fiery orator for freedom during the American Revolution."

A native of Ohio, George worked his way westward through corporations such as Beldon Wire & Cable, Crosley Corporation, Concertone, American Avionics, and eventually LearJet, where he was the general manager. He was a past member of the Young President's Organization, whose membership is restricted to those who have achieved the presidency of a million-dollar corporation before the age of 35. He was a trustee of Azuza Pacific College and Aerospace Components Corporation.

In 1965, George established Bible Voice, Inc., which produced the first complete Bible on long-play records and cassette tapes.

In 1972, High Adventure Ministries was born. During his very active speaking ministry, he began to make numerous trips to the Holy Land. Since 1974, over 6,000 pilgrims have traveled to the "land of the Bible" on High Adventure tours. The pilgrimages provided the "springboard" for special meetings with top Israeli and Lebanese leaders.

In 1973, High Adventure Voice of Hope Radio ministry was launched and soon became a powerful broadcasting world radio network.

In 1979, George met with the late Major Saad Haddad (former commander of Free Lebanon) and took the initiative to build the first Christian broadcasting facility in that region, which is now a part of the Christian Broadcasting Network. Also, High Adventure built the Voice of Hope radio stations on the border of Israel and Lebanon as a way of reaching Jews and Muslims for Christ. This broadcast ministry reached and continues to reach more than 200 countries on every continent. In 1996, High Adventure added a brand new station near Jerusalem.

Dr. George Otis has authored more than a dozen books, including *Voice of Hope*, which describes the birthing of the Voice of Hope Radio Network. See the following page for information on how to obtain your gift copy of this remarkable 210-page book.

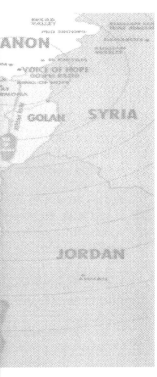

A Daring Mission of Courage and Peace

Voice of Hope

This is the miracle story of a Christian radio station built on the world's most active battlefield, under the ever-threatening PLO fortress — Beaufort Castle — yet protected from those computerized cannons by an army of angels. It is a story of war and terrorism, faith and courage — a story where God's love triumphs over hate and evil.

To get your free copy
of the thrilling book *Voice of Hope* (214p.),
write or call:
George Otis
Box 100
Simi Valley, CA 93062-0100
(805) 520-9460
http://www.highadventure.org

Destiny Image
Revival Books

WHEN THE HEAVENS ARE BRASS

by John Kilpatrick.

Pastor John Kilpatrick wanted something more. He began to pray, but it seemed like the heavens were brass. The lessons he learned over the years helped birth a mighty revival in Brownsville Assembly of God that is sweeping through this nation and the world. The dynamic truths in this book could birth life-changing revival in your own life and ministry!

Paperback Book, 168p. ISBN 1-56043-190-3 (6" X 9") Retail $9.99

WHITE CANE RELIGION
And Other Messages From the Brownsville Revival

by Stephen Hill.

In less than two years, Evangelist Stephen Hill has won nearly 100,000 to Christ while preaching repentance, forgiveness, and the power of the blood in what has been called "The Brownsville Revival" in Pensacola, Florida. Experience the anointing of the best of this evangelist's life-changing revival messages in this dynamic book!

Paperback Book, 182p. ISBN 1-56043-186-5 Retail $8.99

PORTAL IN PENSACOLA

by Renee DeLoriea.

What is happening in Pensacola, Florida? Why are people from all over the world streaming to one church in this city? The answer is simple: *Revival!* For more than a year, Renee DeLoriea has lived in the midst of the revival at Brownsville Assembly of God. *Portal in Pensacola* is her firsthand account of this powerful move of the Spirit that is illuminating and transforming the lives of thousands!

Paperback Book, 182p. ISBN 1-56043-189-X Retail $8.99

Available at your local Christian bookstore.

Internet: http://www.reapernet.com

Prices subject to change without notice.

D *Destiny Image*
Revival Books

LET NO ONE DECEIVE YOU
by Dr. Michael L. Brown.

No one is knowingly deceived. Everyone assumes it's "the other guy" who is off track. So when people dispute the validity of current revivals, how do you know who is right? In this book Dr. Michael Brown takes a look at current revivals and at the arguments critics are using to question their validity. After examining Scripture, historical accounts of past revivals, and the fruits of the current movements, Dr. Brown comes to a logical conclusion: God's Spirit is moving. *Let No One Deceive You!*
Paperback Book, 312p. ISBN 1-56043-693-X (6" X 9") Retail $10.99

THE GOD MOCKERS
And Other Messages From the Brownsville Revival
by Stephen Hill.

Hear the truth of God as few men have dared to tell it! In his usual passionate and direct manner, Evangelist Stephen Hill directs people to an uncompromised Christian life of holiness. The messages in this book will burn through every hindrance that keeps you from going further in God!
Paperback Book, 182p. ISBN 1-56043-691-3 Retail $8.99

IT'S TIME
by Richard Crisco.

"We say that 'Generation X' does not know what they are searching for in life. But we are wrong. They know what they desire. We, as the Church, are the ones without a revelation of what they need." It is time to stop entertaining our youth with pizza parties and start training an army for God. Find out in this dynamic book how the Brownsville youth have exploded with revival power...affecting the surrounding schools and communities!
Paperback Book, 140p. ISBN 1-56043-690-5 Retail $8.99

A TOUCH OF GLORY
by Lindell Cooley.

This book was written for the countless "unknowns" who, like Lindell Cooley, are being plucked from obscurity for a divine work of destiny. Here Lindell, the worship leader of the Brownsville Revival, tells of his own journey from knowing God's hand was upon him to trusting Him. The key to personal revival is a life-changing encounter with the living God. There is no substitute for a touch of His glory.
Paperback Book, 182p. ISBN 1-56043-689-1 Retail $8.99

Available at your local Christian bookstore.

Internet: http://www.reapernet.com

Prices subject to change without notice.

Destiny Image
New Releases

IT'S NOT OVER 'TIL IT'S OVER

by Matthew Ashimolowo.

Do your circumstances seem overwhelming? Are you tired of feeling earthbound when your heart longs to soar? Does your smile merely hide your pain? Have you questioned why you were born? Are you wondering how you can possibly go on? Hang on! Help is on the way! *It's Not Over 'til It's Over!*
Paperback Book, 140p. ISBN 1-56043-184-9 Retail $7.99

THE SHOCK WAVE

by Burton Seavey.

Listen! Do you hear it? The explosion that occurred 2,000 years ago at Pentecost is still reverberating around the world! This next "shock wave" of the Spirit will mature and equip the saints, and sweep vast multitudes into the Kingdom of God—but is the Church ready? Find out how you can prepare in this dynamic book!
Paperback Book, 276p. ISBN 1-56043-283-7 (6" X 9") Retail $13.99

APOSTLES, PROPHETS AND THE COMING MOVES OF GOD

by Dr. Bill Hamon.

Author of the "Prophets" series, Dr. Bill Hamon brings the same anointed instruction in this new series on apostles! Learn about the apostolic age and how apostles and prophets work together. Find out God's end-time plans for the Church!
Paperback Book, 336p. ISBN 0-939868-09-1 Retail $12.99

IN PURSUIT OF HIS GLORY

by S. Bertram Robinson.

How does the rapidly growing Pentecostal/Charismatic movement fit into the larger framework of the Christian Church? *In Pursuit of His Glory* reveals that the baptism of the Holy Spirit is more than "speaking in tongues": it is a baptism into the life and purpose of Jesus Christ. Discover how God's eternal Kingdom can be advanced in you as you seek to know and experience Him. Prepare to be challenged to launch your own attack against the cultural, ethnic, religious, and political forces that now threaten the end-time harvest of souls.
Paperback Book, 256p. ISBN 1-56043-289-6 (6" X 9") Retail $11.99

Available at your local Christian bookstore.

Internet: http://www.reapernet.com

Prices subject to change without notice.

Exciting titles
by Don Nori

THE POWER OF BROKENNESS

Accepting Brokenness is a must for becoming a true vessel of the Lord, and is a stepping-stone to revival in our hearts, our homes, and our churches. Brokenness alone brings us to the wonderful revelation of how deep and great our Lord's mercy really is. Join this companion who leads us through the darkest of nights. Discover the *Power of Brokenness*.
Paperback Book, 168p. ISBN 1-56043-178-4 Retail $8.99

THE ANGEL AND THE JUDGMENT

Few understand the power of our judgments—or the aftermath of the words we speak in thoughtless, emotional pain. In this powerful story about a preacher and an angel, you'll see how the heavens respond and how the earth is changed by the words we utter in secret.
Paperback Book, 192p. ISBN 1-56043-154-7 (6" X 9") Retail $10.99

HOW TO FIND GOD'S LOVE

Here is a heartwarming story about three people who tell their stories of tragedy, fear, and disease, and how God showed them His love in a real way.
Paperback Book, 108p. ISBN 0-914903-28-4 (4" X 7") Retail $3.99
Also available in Spanish.
Paperback Book, 144p. ISBN 1-56043-024-9 (4" X 7") Retail $3.99

Available at your local Christian bookstore.

Internet: http://www.reapernet.com

Prices subject to change without notice.

Other
Destiny Image titles
you will enjoy reading

HEALING THROUGH SPIRITUAL WARFARE
by Dr. Peggy Scarborough.

This practical book is a tool for spiritually warring for healing. Using battle terms, Dr. Scarborough teaches how a believer can fight sickness and win! Well documented, personal, and practical, this book will stir your heart to join the fight against the enemy.

Paperback Book, 210p. ISBN 1-56043-796-0 Retail $8.99

PRAYER AND FASTING
by Dr. Kingsley A. Fletcher.

We cry, "O God...bring revival to our families, our churches, and our nation." But we end our prayers quickly—everyone is hungry and we must eat before our food gets cold. Is it any wonder that our prayers are not prevailing? Fasting and prayer focus your thoughts and sharpen your expectancy so that when you ask, you expect to receive. Discover the benefits of prayer and fasting and learn to fast successfully.

Paperback Book, 168p. ISBN 1-56043-070-2 Retail $8.99

THE PRAYING CHURCH
by Sue Curran.

Churches around the world are responding to the call of God to give themselves to corporate prayer. In this book Pastor Curran addresses the practical aspects of corporate prayer meetings and shares dynamics she learned for effectively leading a "praying church."

Paperback Book, 154p. ISBN 1-56043-250-0 (5" X 8") Retail $7.99

Available at your local Christian bookstore.
Internet: http://www.reapernet.com

Prices subject to change without notice.